20 Questions to Ask

If Your Child Has ADHD

Mary Fowler

Foreword by Scott Eyre, Chicago Cubs

CAREER
PRESS
THE CAREER PRESS, INC.
Franklin Lakes, NJ

20 QUESTIONS TO ASK IF YOUR CHILD HAS ADHD
EDITED AND TYPESET BY GINA TALUCCI
Cover design by Lu Rossman/Digi Dog Design
Printed in the U.S.A. by Book-mart Press

To order this title, please call toll-free 1-800-CAREER-1 (NJ and Canada: 201-848-0310) to order using VISA or MasterCard, or for further information on books from Career Press.

CAREER
PRESS

The Career Press, Inc., 3 Tice Road, PO Box 687,
Franklin Lakes, NJ 07417
www.careerpress.com

Library of Congress Cataloging-in-Publication Data

Fowler, Mary.

20 questions to ask if your child has ADHD / by Mary Fowler.

p. cm.

Includes bibliographical references.

ISBN-13: 978-1-56414-852-2 (paper)

ISBN-10: 1-56414-858-0 (paper)

Attention-deficit hyperactivity disorder Popular works. I. Title: Twenty questions to ask if your child has ADHD. II. Title.

RJ506.H9F67 2006

618.92′ 8589--dc22

2005058103

Dedication

For my dear friend Rivka Arotchas, a wonderfully wise mother and coach who has helped so many families and children with ADHD; and to her husband, Ahron, and their children Reni, Itzak, and Yonatan.

Acknowledgments

Writing this book has been very much like a team sport. Since I first became involved with educating others about ADHD, I've been privileged to play ball with some exceptional people—especially the parents and children with ADHD who have confided in me. Our conversations helped shape the content of this book. Much substance also comes from members of the ADHD research community who have always been generous in educating me so that I could educate others. Without their hard work, advances in the understanding and treatment of ADHD would not happen.

What would a ball game be without a home-team cheering squad? Thank you, Nancy Stromp (for the wonderful working space), Catherine Ricker, Pat Mills, Lynn Hilton, Eric MacKellar, Hal Meyer, Sandy and Russ Thomas, and my family, especially my mother, who waited.

I also thank Mike Lewis (my former Career Press editor) for asking me to write this book, and Michael Pye and Gina Talucci who saw it through until it reached home plate! A grateful salute goes to Steve Alexander for facilitating the foreword by Major League pitcher Scott Eyre.

Last, but most definitely not least, my heartfelt thanks to you, Scott Eyre, for throwing the first pitch in this team effort. Your message empowers us to see the possibilities in life rather than the limitations. Your story reminds us that ADHD struggles can be well met with help and intervention, and that people with ADHD dream, compete, with the best, and win.

Contents

Foreword

My life can easily be divided into "before and after" ADHD. I was diagnosed at age 30 after a lifetime of not being able to focus, sit still, stop talking, complete tasks, and, in general, live the kind of life that "normal" people around me seemed to be living. As a child and teenager, I was hyper, impulsive, restless, and could lose my temper at the smallest things. As an adult pitching in the major league, I easily lost my focus and, at times, all I could hear or see or think about were the noisy stadiums, the fans screaming nasty things about me, the lights, the advertisements, the music, the announcer—everything except what I was supposed to be focused on: my pitching. Sometimes, I'd be able to grab on to something inside me that would pull me back to a point where I could get through it and do my job, but too often, I couldn't.

Gradually, with the help of friends, teammates, and team doctors, I realized there was a name for all of that frustration. Now, medication gives me a chance to learn and practice strategies for staying focused, which allows me to be a better ballplayer, better husband, better father, and just a better person, in general. I can see what I had been missing out on, and what my family, friends, and coworkers had to put up with.

The main reason I share my story is to let kids and parents know that having ADHD is nothing to be ashamed of. It doesn't mean they are bad or defective. It doesn't mean that they can't do good things, feel good about themselves, and have the same dreams as any other kid has about doing great things in the future. Most of all, it doesn't mean that there is no hope.

I'm lucky to have had baseball as I was growing up as a source of success and positive reinforcement. But whether it's sports, art, music, writing poetry, or whatever, each child has something they can be successful at and feel good about, especially if their parents or other significant adults in their lives are supportive.

My mom, without realizing it because no one knew what ADHD was when I was a kid, was doing just what the parent of a child with ADHD should do: she was calm and comforting. She encouraged me. She believed in me. She allowed me the freedom to feel that I could chase my dream of being a major league baseball player. Now that I'm a parent, I have an even greater appreciation for what she did, and still does. I know that I'm a much better parent to Caleb and Jacob since I was diagnosed. And I think that my wife, Laura, will agree that I'm a better husband and that we're a happier family.

While my diagnosis has led to professional success beyond my dreams, the personal achievements within my family life are what I treasure most.

I urge you, as a parent, to embrace the help that's available, including what Mary has to offer in the following chapters. And never lose hope.

SCOTT EYRE
CHICAGO CUBS

Introduction

Dear Reader,

You may find that exploring the subject of ADHD and eating popcorn have a lot in common. Once you start, you keep going. This book provides the first course. I encourage you to continue to educate yourself about ADHD. Eat heartily, but practice good nutrition! Take your information from sources that have been validated by quality research and practice.

For more than 20 years, I have lived, studied, and written about this disorder. The information in this book comes from highly respected researched findings and practice. The book is a primer designed to answer your basic questions, but is not intended to replace professional help. If you, your child, or family is struggling, I strongly encourage you to seek outside help. Use your reading as a basis of self-education—not as a replacement for necessary treatment.

This book is organized into four parts. Questions 1–5 provide general information about ADHD. Questions 6–9 explore social-emotional issues. Questions 10–15 examine home and family problems and strategies. Questions 16–19 cover ADHD and school-related issues, and Question 20 offers guidance for the future. Additionally, Scott Eyre's foreword reminds us that tomorrow is built upon today.

So much can be done to help your child live a well-adjusted life. May this book answer most of your questions, steer you in the right direction, and bring you and your child comfort and support, a sense of balance, and a healthy dose of lightheartedness and hope.

Question 1

What Is ADHD?

If your child has Attention Deficit Hyperactivity Disorder (ADHD), you may be feeling a bit confused, sad, and possibly overwhelmed. You know your child's been having challenges in school, at home, and with other kids. You've probably been having a few of your own. But ADHD? You might not even be sure what that is.

You may have heard a lot of conflicting information. You may secretly believe it's really you—something about your parenting, something you are or are not doing. You may be worried to death about your child and not sure you're up to the challenge. Perhaps you're getting angry with the school. Maybe you're thinking, "They're supposed to be the experts. Why do they keep calling me?" Or maybe you just wish your child would do what the teachers want or expect. Maybe you feel exasperated because you're not sure what to do.

Take a deep breath. Go for a walk. Clear your head. Let go of any thoughts that criticize or blame you or your child. From now on you'll be searching for answers that are helpful and productive. Know that learning to cope with and manage ADHD, whether you are the parent, the teacher, or the child, is a process that begins with kindness and unfolds through knowledge and understanding.

So What Exactly Is ADHD?

Attention Deficit/Hyperactivity Disorder is one of the most commonly occurring childhood disorders. The American Pediatrics Association (APA) estimates that three to seven out of every 100 school-age children have it. ADHD begins in childhood. In most cases, symptoms and ADHD-related issues require attention throughout the teen and adult years.

ADHD is considered a medical/mental health condition. That does not mean your child is "crazy," "seriously ill," or "doomed." A lot of highly creative and successful adults credit their ADHD as the driving force behind their success. They will also tell you that ADHD presented some significant challenges that they faced because they were not properly diagnosed or received the right kind of help. As you seek answers for the questions and solutions for the problems, keep in mind the words of the 19th century philosopher and psychologist William James: "I will act as though what I do makes a difference. It does!"

> *"I will act as though what I do makes a difference."*
> —William James

How Do We Know for Sure It's ADHD?

You may know the Indian fable about six blind men who tried to figure out what an elephant looks like. Each man "looked at" a part of the elephant with his hands. Needless to say, each "saw" something different. The one who felt the animal's side said the elephant was similar to a wall, while the one who felt the trunk said, "The elephant is like a snake." "No," said the others. "It is like a spear (tusk)." "It is like a tree (leg)." "It is like a fan (ear)." "It is like a rope (tail.)" The men could not come to an agreement. Each blind man was so sure that he was right, so they went to a wise man to solve their disagreement. The wise man told them, "You are all right. But you are all wrong, too. For each of you touched only one part of the animal. To know what an elephant is really like, you must put all those parts together."

That's what it's like to diagnose ADHD. The parts must be put together because, presently, there is no surefire way such as a blood test or brain scan to tell. And simple observation, as the blind men learned, isn't too reliable either. So how do you know what you're looking at?

ADHD'S Main Symptoms

There are three main features associated with Attention Deficit Hyperactivity Disorder: attention problems, hyperactivity, and impulsivity. Your child does not have to have problems in all three areas. Sometimes that causes a lot of confusion, especially if, similar to the blind men, you don't know what you're dealing with and you're trying to figure it out piece by piece.

Kids with ADHD come in all sizes and shapes. Yours may be really inattentive but not too hyper— could maybe even use a little oomph! But then you talk with another parent who describes his or her child as super hyper or wildly impulsive. One child may be highly anxious; another aggressive. Some may do well in school—especially in the early years. Others may run into problems the minute they enter the school zone.

How can kids with the same diagnosis be so different? Think of all the colors in the world. Every variation comes from the mixing and matching of the three primary colors: red, yellow, and blue. Sometimes you have a real orangey-red; sometimes

15

rosy pink. Sometimes you get lemony-yellow, or a blue that's purplish. For ADHD, the three primary symptoms blend differently for each child.

Now add secondary colors to the core symptoms—environmental factors such as parents, other siblings, expectations, rules, parenting styles, types of schools, socioeconomic status, and so on. That's why two children with ADHD don't ever seem exactly the same. That's why when you're trying to answer the question of what to do next, you want to be sure strategies are for your child's specific issues and not for some "generic" type of "ADHD kid."

By the way, notice in the last sentence, I just used the expression "ADHD kid." There's no such thing as an ADHD kid. We do have children who happen to have ADHD. That's an important part of the question: *My child has ADHD. Now what?* We don't ever want our children to view themselves as their "disorder." Our children have a challenging condition that can and often does cause a lot of problems in life function. ADHD is not who they are. It is what they deal with. From here on, you will never find me referring to a kid as an "ADHD kid."

> *ADHD is not who they are. It is what they deal with.*

Probable Causes

Although researchers haven't yet unraveled the mystery of the human brain, they do have some very good leads when it comes to understanding what causes ADHD. Symptoms result from brain-based biochemical differences not found in children who don't have the disorder. For instance, studies show that some areas of the brain have less electrical-chemical activity and blood flow. There also appears to be a slight difference in the size of certain brain structures. Not surprisingly, the brain areas and systems indicated are those that help us focus and pay continuous attention, limit motor activity, and control impulse and mood.

These chemical differences appear to stem from problems with certain neurotransmitters (brain chemicals that help cells communicate). With ADHD, the neurotransmitter that seems to be the most involved is dopamine, which is found throughout the brain. Scientists have discovered a genetic basis for part of the dopamine problem that exists for *some* people with ADHD. The neurotransmitter, norepinephrine, seems to be somewhat involved, too. Scientists continue to study other neurotransmitters that are suspect.

No one knows for sure what causes the brain differences in children with ADHD, either. The disorder tends to run in families, so there is a genetic link in some cases. Researchers have also noted a higher incidence of other factors, such as oxygen loss, maternal smoking, head trauma, and lead exposure. While there seems to be a relationship between these other factors, they're not considered causes. Neither is too much television viewing!

So, that's what is now known about the "organic" cause of ADHD. Bear in mind the popular saying: Your biology is not your biography. In other words, your child can have ADHD, but the effects of this disorder may be worse when the biology of ADHD meets life and the social world of relationships, expectations, rules, limits, requirements, and so on. The symptoms can be irritated or irritating, and thus result in more layers of difficulty.

Question 2

How Is ADHD
Diagnosed?

There's a big difference between a relative, neighbor, or teacher telling you they think your child has ADHD because they see some "familiar" signs and having a proper evaluation done by a person trained and licensed to evaluate and diagnose the disorder. Many kids are identified as having ADHD by someone at school, usually because the child's behavior disrupts the class. Teachers will notice that the child's ability to perform to his or her best is interfered with by disorganization, or lack of concentration; not being able to sit still; rushing through work; and so on. You can *suspect* that ADHD might be the cause of these problems, but no one should *assume* it is. Why?

The primary colors, or symptoms, of ADHD—inattention, impulsivity, and hyperactivity—can also be found in other medical and mental health conditions. The distinction between ADHD and coexisting conditions is made by looking at patterns of symptoms. Think of a kaleidoscope. You have the same chips of glass, but it's the way these chips fall into place that create the distinct images. You don't want your child to receive unnecessary treatment or not receive treatment for other conditions.

Who Is Qualified to Diagnose ADHD?

Whoever is doing the diagnosis must know how to figure out when something looks like ADHD and when it *is* ADHD with or without coexisting conditions. That person must also determine the degree to which ADHD symptoms affect your child's functioning. Who might that be? Trained individuals licensed to make medical diagnoses include:

- ➲ Pediatricians or family practitioners.
- ➲ Neurologists.
- ➲ Psychiatrists.
- ➲ Child psychologists.
- ➲ School psychologists.
- ➲ Social workers.

Other individuals, (for example, school nurses, guidance counselors, or child study team members), may participate in, or perform a comprehensive assessment. However, the diagnosis must be made by a licensed practitioner, especially for treatment that involves medication or medical insurance reimbursement.

Note: To find names of qualified professionals, check your local resources: hospital child evaluation units, local schools, parent support groups, or the Web. When you call to make an appointment, first ask the person about his or her qualifications and experience with ADHD.

What the Evaluator Looks For

There are diagnostic guidelines that evaluators follow. These are found in a book used by medical and mental health professionals called *The Diagnostic and Statistical Manual of Mental Disorders*. Evaluators look for patterns that create the following two patterns:

1. Children with not enough attention. When it comes to attention problems, they're looking to see if your child has trouble with not paying enough attention, particularly in areas that do not interest or stimulate him or her. That shows up when he or she misses details, makes careless errors, doesn't appear to listen, can't seem to hold attention for long, doesn't finish tasks, misses directions, loses things, gets distracted easily, tends to be forgetful, or frequently says, "This is boring!"

Note: Children with ADHD may get bored easily, but boredom doesn't cause ADHD. Nor is boredom an attitude problem. It comes from a biological need for stimulation.

2. Children with too much activity and too little self-control. While attention problems tend to come from "not enough stimulation," hyperactivity/impulsiveness issues can be likened to too much activity and too little self-control. A child with these symptoms will be in constant motion to some degree: fidgety, restless, or moving like there's an engine strapped to her back. This child may talk a lot, interrupt others, and blurt out answers before questions are asked. You will often hear words similar to these: "I hate to wait." "What's taking so long?" "Let's go." "NOW! I HAVE TO HAVE IT NOW."

Note: Children and adults with ADHD may actually use motion as a way to arouse themselves to focus attention during things they find dull, boring, routine, or neverending.

ADHD Subtypes

Your child can have one of three subtypes of ADHD: Inattentive type, Hyperactive-Impulsive type, or the Combined Type (Attentive, Hyperactive-Impulsive symptoms).

In the Inattentive type, you will see at least six of the types of behaviors described as "not enough attention." A child with the Hyperactive-Impulsive type will seem to do okay with attention but not activity or self-control. Younger children are more likely to have this type of ADHD, but that's only because no one really expects a young child to pay much attention. A kid diagnosed with the Hyperactive-Impulsive type of ADHD (H/I) must have at least six of the behavioral symptoms. Usually the H/I type becomes the Combined type when the child gets to school and demands for an increase in attention. In the Combined type, the child's behavior is described as "not enough attention" with "too much motor and too little self control."

To have ADHD, your child's symptoms must also:

➲ Be present for longer than six months.

➲ Cause significant problems in at least two of three areas: social, home, or school.

➲ Exist before age 7 (but signs may not be recognized until later).

➲ Be developmentally inappropriate for the child's chronological age.

ADHD is not caused by immaturity.

Common Co-occurring Disorders

Often ADHD is accompanied by other disorders. Sometimes these occur as complications caused by ADHD, and at other times they are separate neurologically based issues. Either way, all problems require treatment.

Common co-occurring conditions are:

Learning Disabilities: Problems with learning due to the way the brain receives, processes, uses, or outputs information. (Some schools consider ADHD a learning disability.)

Oppositional Defiant Disorder: Problems obeying rules; easily frustrated; usually negative; angry-type behaviors; arguing; intentionally annoying others; blaming others.

Anxiety: Feeling tense, irritable, restless, edgy, easily over-whelmed, possibly aggressive, or fearful (especially in social situations or when under pressure).

Depression: Feeling sad, disheartened, and hopeless; having low energy and poor concentration.

Tourette's Syndrome: Uncontrollable motor movements, (such as twitches, repetitive sounds, and more). Symptoms often create a range of psychological issues.

The person doing the diagnosis should give you an in-depth explanation about all the issues your child might have, along with treatment recommendations for all the problems.

The Quality Evaluation

Many medical diagnoses are made by objective tests, such as laboratory tests or brain imaging tests. Presently, no objective test exists to diagnose ADHD, although researchers are working to develop objective measures.

For now, this diagnosis is made on the basis of observable behavioral symptoms. That does not mean that the evaluator has to see your child behaving like he or she has ADHD. In fact, it's possible that the evaluator will not see your child show any of the signs of ADHD—especially if it's the first time they've met. Why? Very often, when a child with ADHD is in a new situation such as meeting a doctor for the first time or being the center of an adult's total interest and attention, that child will be very interested and engaged in what he or she is doing.

Does that mean the child doesn't have ADHD? No. It means that the evaluator should never use one source of information to decide if ADHD is a problem or not. That's where training and experience come into play.

Information the Evaluator Uses

Professional organizations such as the American Academy of Pediatrics and The American Academy of Child and Adolescent

Psychiatry advise clinicians to gather the following pieces of information:

- ➲ A physical examination.
- ➲ A thorough medical history, including family history.
- ➲ A medical examination for physical and neurological information, including developmental information.
- ➲ A comprehensive interview with parents and the child.
- ➲ School information: reports from past and present teachers about learning, performance, and behavior; standardized test scores, any school evaluations, grades and attendance records, and school observations whenever possible.

Many clinicians also want a psycho-educational evaluation, which can be performed by them or possibly by your child's school at no cost to you (see Question 18). This evaluation may include:

- ➲ Observation of the child.
- ➲ Standardized behavior rating scales to be filled out by parents and teachers (and the child when appropriate).
- ➲ Psychological tests to measure IQ and social/emotional adjustment.

Proceed with caution! Some doctors prescribe medication to children without performing a thorough evaluation. They think if the child's behavior improves, then the child has ADHD because the symptoms have been relieved by the medication. That is not good medical practice. Find another doctor.

It's Not Something You Said

In the diagnostic process, you are probably the primary provider of information about your child. You may be feeling uncomfortable about what you said and wondering if you led the doctors like horses to water. Perhaps you're thinking you should have focused more on the sweet things about your child instead of the problems. Perhaps you're seeing or hearing those people who have told you that your child's problems would improve if you were a better parent.

If these thoughts are running through your head, you'll want to get out of that head space as soon as possible. You've been the witness to all that your child experiences. You know in your heart if something's not quite right. Be kind to yourself and know that seeking professional help is proactive, brave, and unselfish. It means you love your child so much that you are willing to do whatever is necessary for your child's well-being.

Question 3

How Do I Put ADHD Into Perspective?

If you are a typical parent, now that you've been told your child has ADHD, there are some days when you might think, "Hey, no big deal." At other times you may worry that ADHD will ruin your child's life. You may wonder what you should tell yourself, your child, and others about what to expect today, tomorrow, and the years ahead.

Ease the Expectations

Coming to terms with a diagnosis is a process. On one hand, it often brings a sense of relief— "Hey, it's not me. It's not my child. It's ADHD." After the initial relief, similar to most parents I know, you probably think you should have known more or done something sooner. You may think or feel that you didn't nurture and protect your child enough. You may feel guilty because at times you've been super angry, used harsh discipline, or called your child names.

You may also feel a sense of loss. ADHD issues can rob joy from childhood and family life. You may have plans, dreams, and expectations. Now you're not so sure what your child's future will bring. And of course, no parent wants to watch a child struggle with any issue, let alone a chronic one such as ADHD. So there's some sadness that usually wears the mask of worry.

Coming to terms with ADHD takes time, skill, practice, and patience. The emotions of guilt, shame, blame, anger, sadness, and worry need to be put to rest. Once you and your child learn how to cope and manage, ADHD issues will improve. Practice forgiveness. It's your action from now on that counts. Meanwhile, be mindful that you don't get on the wrong track.

> *Practice forgiveness. It's your action from now on that counts.*

Super Parent Syndrome (SPS)

There's no such thing as "Super Parent Syndrome." I thought up this "condition" to describe myself (and other parents) who have been known to go into overdrive when their child is diagnosed. There's no one reason why we get this way. We might want to make up for "lost" time, make amends for past mess ups, protect our child from any harm, or ensure that our child has the very best outcome. Like all good intentions, at some point they can lead in the wrong direction—especially for the child on the receiving end.

Why? Well, we "super parents" notice and try to correct every little thing the child does or does not do. A piece of paper is out of place. We tell ourselves, "That's the ADHD! I've got to do something." The child forgets a homework assignment.

We (or the teacher) turn it into a federal case! In a nutshell, SPS means we are on the kid—and others, too—for every little mistake. We may also enlist others such as our child's teachers to do the same!

The hell our intentions create is the place where the child feels like perfection is expected, and that she or he is nothing but one mistake after another. If you are in the grips of SPS, here's how to release:

➲ Back off issues that don't matter.

➲ For issues that do matter, focus on one problem at a time.

➲ Notice, enjoy, and reward all progress.

Super parents can go through hell, too. We can become overly invested in our child's trials and tribulations. When things go well, we're high and feel like, "Wow! My kid's a genius. She's gonna rule the world." Then the child hits a snag, a challenge, perhaps a new developmental stage. Things start to fall apart. We tumble down into the "doom and gloom" mode. To get out of this hell, we need balance and perspective.

Lessons From the Jersey Shore

I don't surf. Still, having spent most of my life on the Jersey shore, I've watched waves and their riders. Both have taught me a lot about balance and perhaps a way to put any adversity into perspective.

Some days the surf is good; other days it's not. Some days, the surfer has no trouble with balance. Other days, even under superb conditions, he can't follow the ups and downs of the curl. On days such as these, the surfer spends a lot of time washed up and wiped out. Fortunately, there are those great sustaining days when the surfer is in great form, or when the sea sends one fantastic ride after another.

That's what to expect with ADHD. Expect the ups, downs, and in-betweens that are part of life. Only with ADHD, when the going gets rough, know that the surf's more like what you'd find in Hawaii or California—much bigger ups and downs, and more roiled water. Surf each wave on its terms. Don't worry about the future. Don't dwell on the past.

ADHD gets managed by the moment each and every day. Focus on solutions for problems as they arise. That way, you get to the causes. Otherwise, you will be managing effects and aftereffects. That's like trying to swim against the tide—it will pull you further out.

Thinking Positively

We all do better when we understand the world as a place of possibility rather than limitation. I don't want to discount the struggles ADHD causes—they can be significant. But I also know that it's important to look for the diamonds in coal.

As many people with ADHD have found, ADHD symptoms can be positive qualities under the right circumstances. For example:

➲ Curious, creative mind, sees things other may miss.

➲ Impulsivity, daring, risk taking, entrepreneurial.

➲ Hyperactivity, high energy, enduring, generative.

Guide your child to make a list (or collage with words, pictures, and symbols) of his strengths and positive attributes. Leave out weaknesses! Put the list or collage where it can be a readily seen reminder.

Talking About ADHD With Your Child

In talking about ADHD with your child, you definitely want to stress that ADHD does not limit choices and potential.

As questions arise, answer with a matter-of-fact tone of voice in words your child can understand. Keep in mind her age. Young children don't need lengthy explanations. Neither do older kids with ADHD. They can understand long explanations, but usually they tune out when someone uses too many words. Short, simple, and sensitive explanations are a good rule of thumb.

Choose your words carefully. They will be a reflection of how you view the disorder. If you see it as gloom and doom, your words will send that message. If you view it as manageable and an opportunity for growth and development, your words will send a message of potential and possibility. Though I'd like to give you a canned speech you can make, I can't. You are you. Your child will pick up on any talk you make that's not your own.

> *Short, simple, and sensitive explanations are a good rule of thumb.*

Your child will also let you know when she wants to drop the subject by changing it or walking away. When your child drops an unpleasant subject, let it rest, unless it absolutely has to be discussed. Remember, you're trying to help the child come to an understanding of what ADHD is on her own terms. Force-feeding seldom works.

Many families find it more helpful if the person who does the diagnosis explains ADHD to the child. That can be especially desirable in situations where the child has had a lot of behavior problems at home. Otherwise you might find the child interprets the diagnosis the way one boy I know did: "ADHD's just another way to call a kid bad."

Should I Tell Others My Child Has ADHD?

The simple answer is yes if the knowledge helps the person help your child. ADHD is really your child's business. Though your child may be too young to know how he or she feels about sharing this information with others, the day will come. We need to be sensitive to how the child interprets the label. We want to protect the child from people who see labels as excuses and differences as difficulties without any positives.

You may find you will want to tell coaches, scout leaders, youth directors, and others close to your child. You will want to tell the appropriate personnel at your child's school if they don't know already. Those people would include the principal, the child's teachers, guidance counselor, school nurse, and the child study team if an educational evaluation is needed. Your child's ADHD diagnosis should be part of your child's school and medical records. (Under FERPA, the Family Educational Rights and Privacy Act, only authorized school personnel may read your child's records.)

Dealing With ADHD Skeptics

There are people who do not understand ADHD. There are people who think it's an excuse. There are people who don't believe it exists. Don't waste your energy being defensive or persuasive, especially with someone who's overly invested in his or her opinion. The following example shows a way to avoid a debate when you absolutely have to be in some type of relationship with a person who discounts ADHD.

Grandma vs. Mom

At a parent workshop, a mother brought the following problem to me: "My mother is telling my son that there's no such thing as ADHD. She tells me that these psychologists are full of it, and that there wouldn't be any problem if I were a better parent. No matter what I say, she just puts me down. It's really affecting my son. How can I get my mom to understand ADHD?"

This mom and I had a long discussion about all of the ways she tried to get her mom to come around. Seemingly, she exhausted the commonsense approaches, such as giving grandma reading material and offering to have her attend a visit to the child's doctors. I could see this mom's point. From where we were standing, apparently nothing could work. Then I had an insight.

On the surface, these two women were sparring over ADHD and parent-rearing practices. But it seemed to me the real problem had little to do with converting Grandma into an "ADHD believer." These women were having a mother/daughter power struggle. The daughter seemed to need approval and validation from her mom, who didn't seem likely to give it. Not having met Grandma, I couldn't say what her deal was. Nonetheless, it didn't matter.

I asked this mom, "What would happen if you did not mention ADHD, and instead you focused on the specific issues and problems your child is having? Would your mom try to help solve those problems?" She replied, "I think so. She already does that sometimes." I told her, "Great! I know it's a drag that she fights you on the ADHD diagnosis, but does she need to believe in ADHD to be helpful?" She replied, "I guess not because she does care and she does try to help in her own way." I told her that is what we were looking for—and it is! Sure it would be easier if the grandmother saw ADHD differently, but getting locked into a power struggle would only make the grandmother less likely to be helpful.

We want to steer conversations to explore solutions, because that approach is likely to remove the emotional charge that fuels debate. Then we can hopefully enroll people to play on our treatment team rather than be the opposing force. If not, we need them to be neutral or to limit contact time, which is a hard thing to do, but the child's well-being must come first.

Question 4

How Is ADHD Treated?

"If I had to have a childhood mental health disorder, I'd pick this one. It's the most treatable," author and researcher Russell Barkley once said to me. He wasn't saying that ADHD is easily dealt with or that it can be cured. In fact, his years of research have shown that the disorder can, and often does, cause lots of problems during the course of life.

You may be feeling overwhelmed by uncertainty about where to begin. You may also be feeling the way many parents do: You've been coping and managing, maybe not well, but you've been trying. Then, you learn about ADHD. An emotional switch gets tripped. Your fear and worry flood to the surface. Just when you need to kick things into high gear, you want to fold. You may even do so for a few days as did an old friend who tells this story: "I was so upset. I went to my mother's house and curled into the fetal position. Then after a few days, I got up, got a grip, and got to work." She set out to learn how to do everything she could to help her child.

Recommended by Leading Experts

Very often when we think about treating a problem, we aim to fix it. That's not the goal with ADHD. This condition requires ongoing management of difficulties and issues. One goal is to "normalize" your child's behavior to the greatest extent possible. Another goal is to help your child grow and develop strengths, talents, and abilities, some of which might exist in part to ADHD. There are two basic treatment approaches for ADHD:

- ⮑ **Environmental approaches:** Make changes in the child's external world so that he functions better and perhaps thrives. That means we adults have to focus less on changing the child and more on what do to help the child make changes and adjustments.

- ⮑ **Pharmacological Approaches:** Use medications that work to reduce the biological core symptoms of ADHD.

The rule of all ADHD management techniques is this: They work when you use them.

The rule of all ADHD management techniques is this: They work when you use them. When you stop using them, the child's functioning usually declines. For comprehensive approach techniques that provide structure, skills, strategies, and supports, medical experts recommend the following:

- ⮑ Ongoing ADHD education for parents, teachers, and the child.

- ⮑ Other necessary environmental supports, including appropriate school programs.

⊃ Medication when indicated.

⊃ Behavior management.

These approaches help us provide structure, skills, strategies, and support. Throughout this book you will learn numerous ways to help your child. Don't get hung up on what works best. Your child is an individual, so there are general guidelines and good old "trial and error" approaches. You must also remember this important fact: when you find something that "works," don't expect it to work forever. Part of the charm of ADHD is the constant opportunity to find and create new approaches.

You and Your Child's Treatment Team

Here's the good news: If you've ever wanted to be the Chief Executive Officer of the corporation of your child, you have arrived! Your job description includes these words: ADHD expert, advocate, decision-maker, problem-solver, case manager, parent, and team-builder.

"How can I do all that?" you ask. The same way many parents have: Learn a lot about the disorder and build your child's support team.

Who Else Might Be on the Team?

⊃ **Mental health professional:** For guidance about ADHD management, parenting, and family issues.

⊃ **Medical doctor:** to prescribe and monitor medication, if needed.

⊃ **ADHD parent/child coach:** To help you and your child find solutions to problems and to develop structure, skills, strategies, and support (not to replace other indicated therapies).

⊃ **Child advocate:** To help mainly with school conflicts. (Many parents become expert advocates as they learn the ropes.)

⊃ **Teachers and other school personnel:** To deal with ADHD school-related issues that often create the greatest problems in the child's world.

⊃ **Your child:** Who will ultimately be self-responsible. To meet, go through, and rise above the challenges, your child needs to know everything all the team members do.

Getting ADHD Educated

Education about ADHD is considered the treatment cornerstone. You'll want to learn as much as you can. Be careful—there's a lot of inaccurate, and even false, information out there.

> *Be careful. There's a lot of inaccurate, and even false information out there.*

Ironically, this disorder (much like our kids), often gets a lot of attention and criticism. It makes headlines frequently. Lots of people voice their opinions, biases, and impressions rather than facts. The treatment of ADHD has attracted a fair number of snake oil sales types, too. You may find it hard to know what or who to believe. Beware of information that sounds too good to be true—especially if it offers the once-and-for-all cure or a new gizmo to diagnos the disorder. Here are some consumer guidelines to follow:

⊃ **Rule 1: Read reliable information.**

Check the source. What are the author's credentials? Does he or she have a bias? Is this author saying something totally different from every other author in terms of facts? If so, be suspicious. I've been reading research and writing about ADHD for 20 years. The basic knowledge has not changed a lot. We know more about the brain, and there are new medications. Otherwise, management strategies have been consistently the same. We have some better understanding of the learning problems caused by the disorder, and medical societies are now asking their members to follow the diagnostic/treatment guidelines that I mentioned in the first chapter. These have been around as the best practices for at least two decades.

➲ **Rule 2: Be wary of the Web.**

It's a blessing and a curse. You can find great information, but there's a lot of flaky stuff, too. Visit reputable sites for your information. How can you tell? Generally the government and organizational Websites are highly reliable. They're not trying to sell you anything either. These would have "dot-gov" or "dot-org" addresses. Following are a few suggested sites that will get you off to a good start:

Government Organizations/Advocacy Organizations

www.nimh.nih.gov

www.chadd.org

www.nichd.nih.gov

www.add.org

www.clinicaltrials.gov

www.nichcy.org

www.help4adhd.org

Two dot-coms that also provide quality information are *www.helpforadd.com* and *www.addresources.com.*

➲ **Rule 3: Don't bite the sensational or misleading media bait!**

The media provides an important service in society. We rely on it for knowledge and information. Many media outlets perform their educational service with great integrity. The information they share is balanced and accurate. We're fortunate to have this resource. Even so, newspapers, magazines, television shows, and radio programs rely on your market share. Headlines are designed to hook you. You can't believe everything you read, see, or hear.

Sensationalists are easy to spot. But how about the sources that come across as informed, reasonable, and right, but are not? How does a parent know what to believe? Get a good core block of information. Fact sheets from CHADD (Children and Adults With Attention Deficit Hyperactivity Disorder) or ADDA (Attention Deficit Disorder Association) and this book are a good start.

Check any info you find against these sources. If there's something new or different, then you know you need to thoroughly check out the source and its accuracy.

Ask questions of the professionals on your team, the ADHD organizations, and other trusted individuals.

Know that researchers want to find the ultimate solution for ADHD and do best by these children. If a groundbreaking approach or cure shows up and is proven to be good and true, the word will get out. There will be no second-guessing. Meanwhile, do what the media should be doing: fact-check.

Other Treatments and Management Strategies

Promising

Many researchers are currently searching for new and better ways to diagnose and treat ADHD. Some promising, but not yet proven, approaches are neurofeedback, computerized cognitive training, fatty acid supplementation (omega-3 and Omega-6), the interactive metronome, and yoga. At this time, these approaches remain controversial. Consider them as complimentary alternative approaches (not cures) to be used in conjunction with proven approaches.

37

Doubtful

Approaches that have been widely touted for ADHD treatment but never proven despite scientific research are diet, high doses of vitamins, biofeedback, chiropractic manipulation, and allergy treatments. Most reputable clinicians and researchers would tell you to use these as medically indicated for other conditions, but not for ADHD treatment.

You need to know that diets don't cause, and therefore cannot cure, ADHD. That doesn't mean you should ignore sensible standards of nutrition. Simply know that elimination diets such as the Feingold and sugar elimination diets that promise an end to hyperactivity have never been proven to work by ADHD researchers.

Q*uestion* 5

?

Does My Child Need Medication?

A mother tells me that when her child's physician suggested that her daughter needed medication, she had a hard time knowing what to do. It so happened the doctor made his recommendation during a week when the pros and cons of giving psychiatric medications to kids headlined the news. She felt so confused. Her daughter's problems had reached crisis proportion. Yet the buzz about medication had this mother fearful that the pills the doctor wanted to prescribe would only make matters worse.

Making Medication Decisions

The decision to give a child medication for ADHD, depression, or any other psychiatric issue is not easy. Though a lot of people may have opinions about what you should do, thoroughly inform yourself. Make rational rather than fear-based decisions. Fully consider the recommendations of your child's treatment professional (assuming you trust the doctor). Also know that not every child with ADHD needs medication. The decision needs to be made on a case by case basis.

The idea behind any medical treatment is to do no harm. Clearly, the benefits must outweigh any risks or side effects. Even with a doctor's recommendation, you may still have doubts about the necessity or safety of medication. How do you decide?

Begin With Accurate Information

Initially, you, similar to many parents, may have trouble figuring out what's best for your child because you've heard a lot of false notions. Here's some that I've come across:

➲ Medication is given to make a bad child good.

➲ The parent or teacher can't manage the child.

➲ There's a conspiracy by drug companies to increase market share.

➲ Researchers need drug money to keep their labs going.

Medication is prescribed to children and adults with ADHD when indicated because it improves their functional impairment.

It is important to remember that medication is prescribed for children and adults with ADHD when indicated because it improves their functional impairment.

I strongly recommend that you visit the NIMH Website at *www.nimh.nih.gov*. Read the following report (under ADHD): NIMH Research on Treatment for Attention Deficit Hyperactivity Disorder (ADHD): The Multimodal Treatment Study—Questions and Answers. The MTA (Multimodal Treatment Study) is the most extensive treatment study ever done. It thoroughly examined all the psychological, social, and behavioral treatments for ADHD. Study participants were given the best of the best from the best. The results, published in 1999, are considered to be the gold standard. According to NIMH MTA Research report, "long term combination treatments as well as medication management alone are both significantly superior to intensive behavior treatments and routine community treatments in reducing ADHD symptoms." (NIMH Website)

Know How ADHD Medications Work

The medications most commonly used for ADHD medical management are two types of psycho-stimulants: methylphenidates and amphetamines. When you understand that ADHD is based on neurological—and not environmental factors—then the effectiveness of stimulant medication therapy makes sense. Medication alters the biologically based problem. The neurological issue that ADHD medications seem to improve is under active and under aroused brain neuro-chemical activity.

You may be thinking: "My child is hyperactive and pays attention to just about everything. How can these be symptoms of underarousal?" Simple.

Picture your child learning to ride a bike without training wheels. She wobbles all over the place, yet works very hard to steady and stay upright. Despite all efforts, your child still wobbles and probably falls. She may need you to lend a helping hand. In a way, you stimulate your child's ability to ride evenly, but she still does the pedaling and makes the decisions about where to ride. That's what stimulant medications do. They give that extra stimulation so the brain can come to attention and stay there, stop, or "even out" the motor ride, and work with impulses rather than be run by them.

Why Stimulant Medications Are Used

Stimulants have been in use for more than 50 years. Unless there seems to be a reason not to use them in a particular case, as of now, doctors prescribe stimulants before other classes of drugs because of their effectiveness and relatively minor side effects. They come in short-acting (lasting between three to five hours) and longer-acting (lasting around six to eight hours) forms. Different medications use different delivery systems. For instance, some are time-released while others are continuous release. Your child's physician should explain which stimulant is being prescribed and why.

The following medication chart and explanatory note comes from the National Institute of Mental Health's Website, *www.nimh.nih.gov*: "The medications that seem to be the most effective are a class of drugs known as stimulants. Following is a list of the stimulants, their trade (or brand) names, and their generic names. 'Approved age' means that the drug has been tested and found safe and effective in children of that age."

Trade Name	Generic Name	Approved Age
Adderall	Amphetamine	3 and older
Concerta	methylphenidate (long acting)	6 and older
Cylert*	Pemoline	6 and older
Dexedrine	dextroamphetamine	3 and older
Dextrostat	dextroamphetamine	3 and older
Focalin	dexmethylphenidate	6 and older
Metadate ER	methylphenidate (extended release)	6 and older
Metadate CD	methylphenidate (extended release)	6 and older
Ritalin	Methylphenidate	6 and older
Ritalin SR	methylphenidate (extended release)	6 and older
Ritalin LA	methylphenidate (long acting)	6 and older

*Author's note: Cyclert is no longer on the market.

One of the major benefits of stimulant medications is how quickly they take effect. Once your child is on the correct dose, an almost immediate improvement in attention, hyperactivity, and impulsive behavior will be seen. Improved judgment, performance, and mood control may also be noticed. The positive effects of medication lead to improved life function and, thus, better outcomes.

> *One of the major benefits of stimulant medications is how quickly they take effect.*

Nonstimulant medications labeled specifically for ADHD have recently come into use. As of this writing, Cephalon Pharmaceuticals is awaiting final FDA approval for Sparlon (modafinil) Tablets (C-IV) for use in children and adolescents ages 6-17. While modafinil is an older medication which has been used for other medical conditions for many years, Sparlon will be the first officially labeled ADHD version. It is chemically different from currently approved stimulant and nonstimulant medications. The tablet form will come in varying dosages.

Atomoxetine (Strattera) is a new nonstimulant medication developed specifically for ADHD. It works on the neurotransmitter norephinephrine. This medication can take a number of weeks to produce effects. You should know that the FDA ordered Strattera's manufacturer to place a "black box" advisory on the packaging to warn patients of possible risks including suicidal ideation in children and adolescents.

I strongly urge you to thoroughly discuss all medication decisions with your child's prescribing physician. Always ask the following questions:

- ➲ How long has this particular medication been on the market?

- ➲ Why has the doctor chosen this particular medication?

- ➲ What do the research studies show about its effectiveness?

- ➲ What are the side-effects?

- ➲ Are there any cautionary labels?

Which Stimulant? How Much? How Often?

There is no way to tell which stimulant medication will work best for your child, if at all. Some trial and error is involved. That's true with many medications prescribed for various medical conditions. Following are best medical practice recommendations made by ADHD experts who research these medications. Recommendations are guides and not intended to replace the judgment of the physician who actually knows the child.

Doctors should prescribe a stimulant medication first unless otherwise indicated (see stimulant chart), and assess the results frequently within the first weeks of treatment.

The dose your child needs does not depend on your child's age and weight. Doctors are advised to start with the lowest dose possible and raise it in small amounts until the child's symptoms show improvement.

If symptoms do not improve after a few adjustments, doctors are advised to try another stimulant before switching to a different class of drugs (unless there are severe side-effects with the stimulants). The NIMH reports that one out of 10 children will not be helped by stimulant medications. How often your child takes medication depends on his or her clinical needs and not a one-size-fits-all dosing regimen.

Side Effects of Stimulants

In general, side effects tend to be mild and often go away during the course of treatment (many within the first couple of weeks). Doctors describe these typical stimulant side effects as "nuisances" rather than major concerns. The most commonly reported are:

- ➲ Trouble falling asleep (change medication dose, or schedule, or add medications that help with sleep).
- ➲ Rebound—symptoms worsen as medication wears off (prescribe a smaller dose before medication wears off or switch from long to short acting).
- ➲ Increased irritability (check for drug toxicity, presence of another disorder, or possible rebound).
- ➲ Height and weight (supplement child's nutrition, take "drug holidays," or switch to nonstimulant).
- ➲ Loss of appetite (adjust meal schedule).
- ➲ Stomachache (take with food).

Drug Holidays

"Drug holiday" is a nonmedical term often used to refer to periods when patients "take a break" from the daily regimen of medication. Your child's physician (hopefully with input from you and your child) may decide to withhold medication on weekends and vacations for a couple of reasons: to take a break from side effects or because the medication doesn't appear to be needed at these times. Should this decision be made, monitor your child's behavior and social interaction to make sure that the cost of being off the medication isn't greater than the benefit.

Do Stimulants Lead to Substance Abuse?

Lots of substances have abuse potential. For instance, cigarettes, alcohol, and pot. Even the whipped cream can in your refrigerator can be abused as an inhalant.

According to the National Institute of Mental Health, the stimulant drugs, when used with medical supervision, are usually considered quite safe. Stimulants do not make the child feel "high," although some children say they feel different or funny. Such changes are usually very minor. Although some parents worry that their child may become addicted to the medication, to date there is no convincing evidence that stimulant medications, when used for treatment of ADHD, cause drug abuse or dependence. A review of all long-term studies on stimulant medication and substance abuse conducted by researchers at Massachusetts General Hospital and Harvard Medical School found that teenagers with ADHD who remained on their medication during the teen years had a lower likelihood of substance use or abuse than did ADHD adolescents who were not taking medications. (NIMH Website)

Other Types of Medication Used

Stimulant medications work for the majority of but not all, children with ADHD. Some children will need different types of medications not specifically labeled for ADHD. Other children may have additional disorders that also require medication management, so they may take multiple medications.

These other medications fall into different drug classes:

- ➲ Tricyclic antidepressants.
- ➲ Selective serotonin reuptake inhibitors (antidepressants).
- ➲ Other antidepressants.
- ➲ Antihypertensives.

If your child needs medication other than the stimulants, you will want to consult with an expert. Be sure to find out:

- ➲ What the medication is being used for.
- ➲ Safety and side effects.
- ➲ How long before there's an improvement.

Note: A very helpful parent resource is Timothy Wilens's book, *Straight Talk About Psychiatric Medications for Kids, Revised Edition.* New York: Guilford Press, 2004.

Practice Medication Safety

Monitor Medication

Before your child is placed on medication, the doctor should have you fill out a behavior rating scale to determine the type and severity of your child's symptoms. During the course of treatment, the medication's effectiveness should be assessed. Discuss the best way to monitor medication effects with your child's physician. He or she may recommend a behavior rating scale or specific monitoring system. Or you can visit *www.helpforadd.com* and download the ADHD Monitoring System. Show it to your doctor—it is good for both home and school use. Be sure to look for positive medication effects and not just problems.

Safety Considerations

Discuss the appropriate use of medications with your child. (Never loan medications to others; take as directed; report any side effects.)

- ➲ Don't give your child easy access to the medications.
- ➲ Keep count of the pills.
- ➲ Watch as your child takes the medication.
- ➲ Have in-school doses administered by appropriate school-based personnel.
- ➲ Monitor effectiveness with an objective tool, similar to a rating scale.
- ➲ Communicate all concerns to the prescribing physician.

➲ Keep regularly scheduled doctor appointments. (Experts recommend that blood pressure, heart rate, height, and weight be checked at least two times a year.)

3 Important Medication Facts

1. Stimulant medications do not cure the disorder. They work when they are taken. Symptoms reappear when meds wear off. (Over time, a child's symptoms may improve with brain development and skill gains made from interventions.)

2. Pills don't teach skills. Medications should never be the only treatment used. Children still need structure, skills, strategies, and support that comes from well-designed school, home, and social programs.

3. 80 percent of children who need medication for ADHD will need it as teenagers. About half of them will need meds in adulthood. (NIMH Website)

Doctor Do's and Don'ts

➲ Visit a doctor who specializes in ADHD.

➲ Don't play doctor. Consult the doctor before stopping or changing your child's medication doses.

➲ Check with your pharmacist before giving your child other medications or over-the-counter remedies.

➲ Find a doctor you trust who makes time for your questions and concerns, and who works with you and your child's teachers.

Question 6

Why Is My Child So Emotional?

Many children with ADHD, especially those with hyper-activity/impulsivity, are excessively emotional and overreactive. Their moods may shift like sudden summer storms—the clouds rapidly build, and, like filled-to-the-brim clouds, kids with ADHD often burst.

Your child doesn't mean to be short-fused and temperamental. Nor does your child want to drive people away. Your child's mood management difficulties stem from the way ADHD affects the brain. The disorder makes it harder for children to manage their emotions thoughtfully and with restraint.

The ADHD Neural Highway

The brain system responsible for thoughtful, problem-solving approaches is the executive network. Think of this network as being similar to a super-transportation system with numerous highways, byways, clovers, and exit ramps that connect with all the other brain networks.

Think of ADHD as potholes in the executive network. Though your child may try to be nonreactive, because ADHD affects the brain's executive network, she will have a harder time responding thoughtfully instead of reacting emotionally. The seemingly smallest thing can and often does set her off. That's because the brain's limbic system, which is the quick-fire response network, appears to react before the executive system has a chance to "think." Once again, biology rules!

Understand that the overreactions of children with ADHD are not pre-planned events. For most of us with or without ADHD, loss of emotional control usually results in inappropriate behaviors. With ADHD, inappropriate behaviors may be more extreme and more frequent. Your child may swear, hit, run, scream, or break things. Of course, that type of behavior usually evokes a lot of negative feedback. Plus, these children often get a new adjective: aggressive.

> *The overreactions of children with ADHD are not pre-planned events.*

ADHD's Triple A's—Anger, Anxiety, Aggression

Are children with ADHD aggressive by nature or more prone to aggression as learned behavior? Research hasn't yet answered this question. But I'm inclined to believe that much of the aggressive behavior seen in these children has roots in anxiety. Because kids with ADHD have a biologically based problem thinking things through, they may perceive more of the things that happen as threats. Like stressed-out drivers, they may get nervous and jumpy.

We know that the brain's response to threat is a quick reaction out of fear: fight, flee, or freeze. Anger and aggression can be seen as fighting behavior or a way to avoid or deflect something in the background that may seem threatening. Aggressive behavior may be a maladaptive coping skill learned over time, and which gets reinforced because it works in the moment, similar to a pressure release valve—when overused, it may blow a gasket.

Unintended Consequences

Think of the world of a many a child with ADHD. You have the collision of environmental expectations and ADHD biology, which is not in sync with the expectations. What happens over time compares to a multi-car pileup on a superhighway. Start with the core ADHD issues. Add the emotional over-reactive piece. Then factor in the frequent negative feedback, criticism, rejection, and subsequent frustration of not being able to please, and you may wind up with a heck of a mess.

Research shows that approximately two-thirds of all children with ADHD develop some form of anxiety disorder. Almost half develop Oppositional Defiant Disorder (ODD). ODD is defined as "a recurrent pattern of negativistic, defiant, disobedient, and hostile behavior toward authority figures." When there is no helpful intervention and the child/authority figures continue to clash, half of these children with ODD may go on to develop conduct disorder, which may put them on a juvenile delinquent-type path. Understand that this is a possibility not a probability. Seek expert treatment.

Changing Beliefs

For the kid who is in constant fight, flight, or freeze mode, aggressive, avoidant behavior becomes a pattern. When a child behaves aggressively, it becomes hard to read the emotional substory. Usually this child feels scared and threatened. If your child is often aggressive and angry, you may find it very helpful to realize that your child's behavior probably stems from anxiety. The other people who deal with your child need to know this as well. This shift in belief can make a great positive difference in your child's outcome. Here's why.

Our response changes when we see a child as anxious rather than as aggressive or a bully. We become empathetic rather than punishing and condemning. We tend to tone down our interactions and look for ways to soothe the other. We look for solutions rather than blame and shame. We don't provoke as much.

I'm not suggesting that aggressive behavior be accepted or excused. You and others must take action. That action, however, needs to come from a thoughtful, nonreactive place. After each tense situation, ask yourself these two questions: Did I make it better or worse?Did I respond with thought and restraint?

Changing behavior requires a lot of on-the-spot awareness to plant the seeds for the next time. Learn yourself. Then make a conscious effort to act, rather than react. (This method will work with your child, too.)

Anger as Self-arousal

For some kids with ADHD, anger is a self-arousal strategy. It gets the juices flowing so they can gear up to meet the demands of a situation. This strategy is not something they consciously plan. Rather, they may unconsciously learn it over time the way we all learn habits of mind.

In these cases, children need to learn appropriate ways to self-arouse. Teach your children to deep breathe (see Question 7 on how to do so), fiddle with objects, or use movement such as stretching and yawning as substitute behaviors.

Managing Anger

A lot of kids with ADHD easily fly off the handle. Many are also out of touch with body sensations that signal a build up. Understand that anger, like all emotions, has a range of intensity moving from annoyed, irritated, and angry, to furious and enraged. Once your child reaches the midpoint, it may be very hard for him or her to turn it down. To help your child with anger management, try the following technique:

Draw a thermometer. Write the different degrees of anger (annoyed, irritated, and so on) alongside it. Have your child identify the bodily sensations and behaviors that signal:

⮕ The "I'm starting to lose it" point.

⮕ The "turn-around before it's too late" point.

⮕ The "lose control" point.

Make a list of temperature adjusters (things he can do to cool down before the lose control point) with your child, including blowing raspberries, deep breathing, hopping in place, going for a walk, or leaving the scene. (Make a list with your child.)

As your child begins to work with the thermometer, coach the child to use it more and more until he becomes comfortable with it. You might even keep copies of it posted around the house that everyone can use.

You might also find yoga, ta'i chi, and other forms of conscious movement helpful for you and your child. These activities quiet the nervous system, improve concentration, and increase awareness of bodily sensation. In time, your child (and you) will recognize the "feel" of bodily sensations that signal anxiety, tension, and anger arousal.

Improving Emotional Control

The child developmentalist Erik Erikson believed that four factors help ease children through developmental stages: safety, trust, constancy, and predictability. When we change what we do and deliberately design our child's world with these four factors in mind, we create a more structured and soothing environment. Under these conditions, your child's reactive responses may simmer down.

Safety

Think of safety as the absence of threat. How can you add safety to your child's world?

➲ Prepare the child for changes in advance. Involve your child in plans and preparations.

➲ Limit surprises as much as possible—even spontaneous fun stuff because ADHD children get hyped up by surprise. Do something soothing immediately after a surprise.

➲ Stop reactive behavior, such as yelling, hitting, name calling, and so on. Deep breathe first, and then speak.

➲ Try not to criticize or use other forms of negative feedback.

➲ Keep calm in the wake of an outburst.

➲ Use lots of praise that's meaningful to the child. Catch the child being good!

➲ Respect your child's feelings. Respond to inappropriate actions but acknowledge the feeling behind bad behavior. Teach replacement behavior.

➲ Play with your child. (Nonteaching types of games work best such as shooting hoops, building with blocks, and hide and seek.

➲ Think of other ideas to create safety for your child on a daily basis.

Trust

Think of trust as knowing you can rely on someone else's integrity, ability, and character. How can you help your child develop trust in others?

➲ Do what you say you are going to do. Your child will learn your word is bond.

➲ Think before you act. Your child will feel safer.

➲ Be fair and consistent. Your child should be able to predict your behavior.

➲ Listen with interest and attention, not half an ear.

➲ Show up for extra curricular activities. Interest shows the child you care.

➲ Admit when you've made a mistake. You will teach your child to learn from mistakes by being thoughtful about them—not fearful of them.

➲ Tell the truth even if it's painful. You will teach your child to trust in his or her ability to handle the full range of life situations.

➲ Think of other ways to build trust.

Constancy

Think of constancy as staying the course the way a ship does even in high seas. What principles and operating procedures can you put into place to provide stability?

➲ Have a daily routine: meals, bed, homework, and other activities should take place at the same time each day.

➲ Model and use manners and other social skills.

➲ Make rules that don't change according to your mood.

➲ Show appreciation to your child for following rules. Give hugs, kisses, and nice words.

- ➲ Create routines for organization. (Have the same place for shoes, coats, and backpacks.)
- ➲ Say what you mean, and mean what you say.
- ➲ Have a united parent position.
- ➲ Think about how else can you help your child experience a sense of constancy in her day-to-day world.

Predictability

Think of predictability as something you can count on , such as the sunrise and sunset. What can you do so that your child knows what to expect?

- ➲ Make expectations clear.
- ➲ Act; don't react.
- ➲ Have preset consequences (positive and negative).
- ➲ Do what you say you are going to do.
- ➲ Use contracts and behavior charts.
- ➲ Be consistent.
- ➲ Limit surprises as much as possible. Even well-intended ones such as a spontaneous trip to an amusement park may spark hyper reactivity.
- ➲ Try and come up with other ways that would add predictability to your child's world

Using the Lists

When we change what we do, we create a supportive environment that helps our children change. The previous lists are guides. They may work great for your child and your family. They may be very helpful if used by your child's teachers, too. Like all lists, these need to be looked at and practiced numerous times before they become habit.

Here's the take-home point: Know that your child will be better able to manage ADHD when there are structure, skills, strategies, and supports in place that are used fairly consistently both at home and in school. These lists touch all those bases. In the meantime, try the following suggestions:

- ➲ Make a copy of each list.
- ➲ Each week, choose one category: safety, trust, constancy, or predictability.
- ➲ Each day, practice one principle from that category.
- ➲ Each evening, take stock of how you did.
- ➲ If you did well, praise yourself and move to another principle.
- ➲ If not, practice the same principle the next day. Take note of any improvement.
- ➲ Move on to another principle.

Question 7 ?

What Can I Do About My Stress?

Most parents find raising a child somewhat stressful. Add ADHD. Wow, the stress really increases. You may find that you sometimes or even frequently feel worried, frustrated, over-whelmed, reactive, tired, anxious, angry, guilty, depressed, or sad. I know I did. At times I felt like a basketcase! There were other times (when I had some energy left) when I wanted to run away, which would have been futile. No one can run away from stress.

Here's what I've learned: Stress is a part of life, neither good nor bad. It simply is. What it does is another story. The outcome depends on how we handle it. We don't want to stand in heavy surf and let the waves pound us to pieces. Stress eliminators and management techniques work.

Use It or Lose It!

If you are like I was, you may look at stress management as a luxury item on a long list of "to do's"—the low priority to be used only when you're about to go over the edge. I didn't understand that stress management is not about going on vacation or spending sprees. It's a way of being in daily life. It's no luxury. Few of us can't afford to live without it.

Is It All in Your Head?

A lot of the stress we experience finds its roots in our minds and its expression in our bodies. Excessive stress shows up as symptoms that can be divided into four categories:

- ➲ Physiological: Blood pressure, heart rate, headaches, and muscle tension.

- ➲ Emotional: Anxiety, worry, fear, anger, and depression.

- ➲ Cognitive: Trouble concentrating, forgetfulness, and a drop in performance.

- ➲ Behavioral: Using substances, lashing out, swearing, and being critical.

Look at the categories. Circle the symptoms that apply to you. Add others that may not be listed. These symptoms are your instant messengers. As you first experience a symptom, do an instant replay. Identify its trigger (often worry, fear, or doubt), and eliminate or make peace with this trigger if possible. (It usually is possible, especially if you're willing to be creative.) Following are some additional ways to quiet your body and mind.

Getting a Grip on Stress

See the Problem for What It Is

We have to learn to separate our child from her ADHD. You have a child with a unique personality, interests, and temperament. Separating the child from her behavior creates a perceptual shift that puts us into a less reactive, more problem-solving mode. Less reactivity means less stress. It also helps us accurately define problems instead of perceptions of problems.

What Can You Do?

When your child behaves inappropriately, check your responses and reactions. Are you emotionally engaged in a negative way? Are you separating the child from the behavior? Is your body beginning to tense?

Immediately pull out of this thought pattern. Go for a walk and look at trees or count cracks in the sidewalk. If you have to deal with the behavior, tell yourself, "Act, don't react. It's not my kid. It's the ADHD."

When your child behaves appropriately, check your responses and reactions. Are you emotionally engaged in a positive way? Are you recognizing his positive qualities?

As soon as you notice something good, stop what you are doing. Pay immediate positive attention. Smile and look at your child's eyes. Let him know you're pleased. You'll feel happier, too.

When a problem arises, do you flood with worry, fear, and confusion? A stress reduction teacher I know says, "Tell your mind to shut up." Step back. Breathe some deep breaths. Clear your head. Clarify the problem. Look for solutions, not complications.

Identify the Problem

Identify thought patterns, perceptions, attitudes, and beliefs that create stress. We become reactive to situations that we don't know how to handle or can't control. We create habits of mind. We may perceive things to be larger than life—more than we can handle. We may believe that nothing we try will really work. We may be worn down and worried.

What Can You Do?

Get a grip on worrying. Here's the scoop. We worry because it is an action. It tricks us into believing we are "doing" something about the issue, especially when we don't know exactly what to do and are afraid to take a risk. No magic here. Worry has a habit of making mountains out of molehills. Our goal is to make molehills out of mountains.

Ask yourself, "What can I do besides worry?" If there's no answer, do something constructive to distract yourself. Go for a walk. Make a new dinner recipe. Call someone and brainstorm. Solve an easy problem. The idea here is: Do, don't stew.

Train your brain to see possibilities instead of limitations. Whenever you find yourself in a negative thought, immediately find its positive counterpoint. Ask yourself, "Am I looking for complications because I'm used to living with stress and negativity?" Then think, "What's the flipside? Where's the possibility?" For example, suppose your child forgets to bring homework home. You can take advantage of the situation and realize this is an opportunity to problem-solve, or you can make a federal case out of it and be miserable. Thoughts! Actions! Problem-solving or problem-making? You decide.

> *Train the brain to see possibilities instead of limitations.*

Challenge beliefs and patterns that don't serve you or your child. Many of us feel like we are not very good at being parents. We may secretly believe that others know better. While others can give us guidance and counsel, ultimately we have to live with the decisions we make. We must be our child's champion. So, for example, if you find yourself at a school conference and teachers are telling you that your child's deliberately not doing what she is supposed to, don't become apologetic, defensive, or angry with your child. Ask the teachers what they are going to do to help your child deal effectively with the problem. Remember, you're not looking to make excuses. You're solution-focused, not blame and punishment-driven.

Change the emotional substory. Every story has two strands: the fact pattern and the emotional substory. In the story of your child and ADHD, do you think the worst or expect the best? Do you believe your child can, will be, and is being helped? Do you believe your child will be able to weather life's ups and downs? Do you reflect confidence and positive beliefs?

Immediately change any negative beliefs you notice. They drain your energy, make you miserable, and set a bad example for your child. (Recall the homework example a few paragraphs earlier.) You can train your brain to think positively and productively.

Remember, you are a powerful mirror and your attitude creates an important reflection. Make your attitude positive and optimistic. It will rub off on your child and encourage him or her to move beyond the adversity.

These mental or cognitive reframing methods work over time. They take practice. They will create the positive changes that eliminate or put your stressors into perspective. Use them! Eventually you will see a difference. You may even find your child falls into step.

Stress Reduction Techniques

The expression "We reap what we sow" certainly applies to the way stress affects us. If you're stressed out and don't practice methods to calm down, expect your body to stay in an elevated stress mode. Eventually, you will develop stress-related illnesses. You don't want any of these, so work on making meaningful mental shifts and on soothing your body and mind with the following techniques.

Breathe

Signs of too much stress are rapid or shallow breathing and holding your breath. Be mindful of your breathing throughout the day. When you listen to and feel the movement of the breath, you are "thinking" about it, and not about what's bothering you. Every once in a while simply pause and take a "breath check." Are your breaths deep and slow?

Deliberately fill your lungs with long, slow inhales and exhales equal in length, if not longer. Breathe into the lower part of your lungs. Your abdomen will automatically rise. Try it right now!

Concentrate just on your breath, on the air as it fills your lungs, and the rise and fall of your stomach. This is called following the breath. If it's hard to do, try counting as you breathe in and out: 1...2... 3... 4... 5... 6... 5... 4... 3... 2...1.

Do this until you calm down—at least five minutes. Also, do it whenever you can as a preventative. (Some people think about a peaceful scene or repeat a soothing word as they breathe, rather than count.)

Focus

Fortunately, the brain cannot think of two things at exactly the same time. When you focus on something else, the racing thoughts and worries will stop. Repetitive activities also work well: jog, walk, knit, or intentionally pace. When doing these, pay attention only to what you are doing at that very moment. If a bothersome weedy thought comes into your mind, let it pass or clip it!

Personal Favorites

Our hobbies and interests are great stress reducers. Use them. You can create or listen to music, paint, cook, sew, garden, clean, golf, or do yoga. Right now, stop reading. Get out your pen. Write down what you like to do. Schedule time to do it! No excuses.

If you've totally lost touch and can't remember or are not even sure you ever knew what you truly enjoyed, jot down things you might try—even the far-out ideas: training for a marble shooting contest, learning to play the tin whistle, and so on.

Meditation

Meditation is a structured and daily scheduled practice for quieting the mind that requires some training. There are different forms of meditation. You don't need to travel to the Himalayas to learn how to meditate. I coach my clients in it and other stress reduction techniques on the phone or in person. You can go online to find a place near you that trains meditation. Or you can learn by using books or tapes.

For meditation to be effective, you will want to do it at least once if not twice a day for at least 20 minutes. At first most people think, "Where can I find that kind of time?" or "I can't start my morning that way!" Talk to anyone who's meditated for awhile. Guaranteed that person will say something such as, "I don't know how I lived without it!" or "I wouldn't think of letting anything interfere with my meditation time."

Don't Become a Stress Statistic

As parents with busy lives, we are sometimes reluctant to give ourselves the time we need to de-stress. Perhaps we don't think we deserve the time, or we're too tired, overwhelmed, or just in a funk. Working on your stress health is not a luxury: it's a necessity. The quieter and more in control you are, the better off your child will be. Remember, it's not all about the child with ADHD. This disorder affects the entire family. Pay attention to the stress it creates so it does not rob your joy and peace of mind or make you physically ill. Do that, and you will be a better parent.

Question 8

How Can I Better My Child's Sense of SElf-Worth?

Some children with ADHD come to see themselves as having little to offer. In part, this deficit viewpoint arises out of their struggles with meeting daily performance expectations. But I dare to say, probably the greatest drain on psychological well-being is the way others relate to these children. Rather than empathy and compassion being the day's nectar, they often swallow a lot of potent, unpleasant tasting stuff.

How Does It Feel to Have ADHD?

Let's say you want to get a glass of water. This goal seems very easy to accomplish. But suppose you are in a desert or 3 years old and can't reach the faucet? Not so easy then, is it?

Now, let's suppose you have ADHD. You are on your way to getting the water but you get distracted by something else. You end up forgetting to get the water or take much longer than someone else would. As a consequence, you may run out of time to do something else you need to do or get yelled at for "taking so long." Others might judge your actions and accuse you of deliberately procrastinating.

If you're in school, the teacher might think you're interested in socializing, wanting to get out of work, or trying to create a disruption. She might even take it personally, as if your main goal in life is to drive an adult crazy. The teacher may yell and say, "You will never be allowed to drink water in school again."

If you're at home and it's bedtime, your parents might think you are trying to avoid going to bed. They may get annoyed or totally aggravated. "But it's just a glass of water. What's the big deal?" you think. Over time, you learn that It's never just a simple glass of water; it's always something good intended but gone wrong. You come to believe it isn't what you are or are not doing that ticks them off—it's YOU!

> *You come to believe it isn't what you are or are not doing that ticks them off—it's YOU!*

This water example may seem silly or insignificant. But if you are a child with attention and inhibition problems who's constantly off the mark, a glass of water becomes just one of many drips that make a damned life. You get too much criticism, judgment, negative feedback, misattribution, and assumptions about your behavior—it's deliberate, willful, and *intentional*.

Kids with ADHD (and adults, too) have a hard time separating the best of intentions from messed up executions. They often become very hard on themselves.

I've used a glass of water as an example. We could just as easily be talking about homework, chores, a conversation, or a social game. The list is as big as daily life. It is the measure between knowing the rules and environmental expectations and being able to focus, inhibit, and follow them. It is the collision of a biological problem with a world that doesn't understand— a world that judges and punishes.

How Best Intentions Go Awry

Kids with ADHD are not the only ones who may have great intentions but poor execution. In the daily interactions of the social world, it's easy for adults to stray from how we truly wish to relate to others, especially with children who suffer from behavioral disorders. We get caught in the stresses, the beliefs of how things should be, and the misattributions we make about their behavior and their intentions. Fortunately, it doesn't take a lot of grace to bring us back to our best intentions. Craziness will get you there!

Be Crazy About Your Child

The good news about self-concept is that it is fluid and dynamic. Like the sea, it rises and falls with the changing tides of feedback and life experience. The child with ADHD who develops a negative self-image can turn this perception around, especially when he receives positive feedback and experiences success.

In his book *A Sense of Self*, my author-friend Tom Cottle brought these words of Eli Newberger to my attention: "Every child needs one adult in life who is crazy about him." Be crazy about your child. Pay attention to what he does well. Structure opportunities for him to shine in desired ways.

Put this book down and take out your pen. Make a list of your child's positive qualities. They are the building blocks for your child's new story.

How to Change Self-Stories

Recreate Beliefs

Belief systems create self-stories. If your child is invested in a negative self-script, a lot of your child's positive qualities can be used to revise it.

- ⊃ Look over the list of your child's positive qualities.
- ⊃ Create or support places where your child can use them.
- ⊃ Give lots of deliberate positive feedback.
- ⊃ Enlist others to pay attention to your child's saving graces. How? Share your list with them. Ask them to add to it. Then you both can monitor how much positive attention you pay.

Try this: Put a handful of pennies into your right pocket. Every time you pay positive attention, move a penny to your left pocket. At day's end, hopefully all your pennies will be "spent." (And hopefully you've started out with a sizeable amount, such as 25 pennies instead of just one or two.)

> *"Every child needs at least one adult in life who is crazy about him."*
>
> —*Eli Newberger*

Use the Power of Ordinary Magic

Children are amazingly resilient. Under the right conditions, they can bounce back from adversity. Fortunately, children who are down on themselves don't need Harry Potter's wizardry to get right-side up. According to resilience researcher Anne Masten, "ordinary magic" works wonders. Your child needs:

- ⊃ Caring, competent parents. Because you are reading this book, you care. Because you're learning how to manage ADHD, you're building competence, too.

- ⊃ Connections to other competent caring adults— potential champions. It takes a village to raise a child with ADHD. Look to the resources in your child's life: teachers, coaches, relatives, neighbors, and friends.

➲ Problem-solving ability. Your child will be developing this skill while learning how to live with and manage ADHD.

➲ Belief in your capabilities. Belief will grow out of each success experienced, especially when you use positive feedback to train your child's eyes to see what he does competently.

➲ Talents your child and society value. You and your child will unearth these as you explore ways to put strengths and positive qualities into play.

Positive Doings

Give Affirmation

There are a number of ways you can help your child see possibility and promise. Understand that building this mindset takes consistent behavior over time on your part.

Use Praise

Your child will appreciate and take to heart your glowing words provided that she feels they are authentic and meaningful. Use a lot of praise, but be careful. We parents have a tendency, when we see our kids feeling badly, to try too hard to praise them. Praising just for the sake of praising can be interpreted by the child as "I'm so lame that's all they can find to say about me." Also, kids who are really down and perhaps hostile tend to reject praise. In these cases, still give it, but tone it down and wait a few minutes after they've done something praiseworthy to comment. Let it soak in, but don't expect a positive response—at least not immediately.

Love and Connect

Interest is one of the most powerful positive emotions. Showing interest in our children's interests, comings, and goings is a powerfully positive way to connect. Spend time together and listen to your child. Be mentally present when you are physically present. Be actively engaged and not just on autopilot.

Nurture Your Family

Warm, loving, good times make the glue that binds families. A lot of parents with ADHD avoid family times because there's more opportunity for conflict. When not structured properly, family times can turn into nightmares. If you know sitting and waiting for meals at restaurants rattles your child, plan around that. The idea is not to avoid such situations, but to add structure. Keep it simple. Because your child most likely doesn't stick with things too long, short and sweet may be a good rule of thumb. Think a minute: What nurtures and sustains your family? Add more of it.

Build Community Connections

Put your child's energy and distractibility to work. Volunteerism is a great way to get your child involved in positive, affirming activity.

Work With Your Child's Strengths and Interests

Every child has strong areas. These areas are sources for positive feedback both from others as well as the child himself. The idea here is to focus on what your child does well and not on perfection or being number one. Maybe your child likes to run. Enroll him in local running races where the kudos come from finishing, not finishing first. If the first-place finishes happen, hey, that's added grace.

Stop reading. Make a list of possibilities. What attracts your child? What areas of competence does she or he have? If you're not sure, explore and experiment. Interests and affinities can be sorted into five basic categories:

- ➲ Artistic or creative skills.
- ➲ Social skills and contacts.
- ➲ Sports and recreation.
- ➲ Academic knowledge or skills.
- ➲ Relaxation and fun.

Wise Practices

You may be thinking, "How can I do all of this? I barely have time to cope as it is!" That's one of those negative beliefs. In essence, you aren't doing more, you're just changing your perspective and what you pay attention to. Chances are you already spend a lot of time engaged in nonproductive circular arguments and behaviors that get you nowhere and make everyone feel badly. Once you make the conversion to a positive, problem-solving focus, you'll be spending the same amount of time (probably less) in arguments, only in a much more pleasant way.

Meanwhile, you can begin with small steps. Your child will come to like herself better when she feels valued and appreciated. As parents and community members, we have words of wisdom we can follow that are guaranteed to bring positive results when used consistently.

Have your *"eyes light up"* when you see your child (Maya Angelou). *Smile* because "when you smile at me, you know I will understand. That is something everybody, everywhere does in the same language" (the song *Wooden Ships*).

Let the first greeting you give your child be a genuine smile. Try it. You'll see your child warm up—maybe not the first time, particularly if she is especially down, but over time, a change will happen. I've seen it with my own eyes!

Question 9

How Can I Help My Child's Social Skills?

The Navajo have a saying: "Pray in the morning if you intend to set out alone." For many children with ADHD, the social world can be a lonely landscape or a rugged trail. Children with ADHD don't deliberately choose to set out alone in the social world. Similar to all children, they want to be loved, appreciated, accepted, popular, and have a chance to participate.

Sadly, many kids with ADHD get branded by their behavior. Peers tend to see their ADHD characteristics in a negative light. As you may know, these children experience a lot of social difficulties, especially isolation and rejection. Often they're clueless as to why. As parents, our hearts hurt for them.

We also have reason for concern. Statistics show that children with significant social difficulties are at risk for substance use and abuse, poor peer selection, and bullying or victimization. We, as parents, want to do all we can to protect our children from social harm.

Why ADHD Creates Social Difficulties

Social Basics

We enter into social relationships because they benefit us in some way. Though there is no written code of traits that define desirability, most kids tend to be attracted to other children who have self-control and who accurately read the social pulse—usually not ADHD strengths. There are unwritten rules, too:

- ➲ Play nice.
- ➲ Share.
- ➲ Wait your turn.
- ➲ Follow the social barometer (mood and setting/situation expectations: a church service versus a birthday party).
- ➲ Respect boundaries.
- ➲ Know and follow the rules of the game.

> *Most kids tend to be attracted to other children who accurately read the social pulse.*

Look over this list. No wonder children with ADHD have more than their share of social difficulties. While these "unwritten" rules serve as social guides and many people make social "mistakes" from time to time, the rules often go unnoticed and unheeded for kids with ADHD. Mistakes tend to be more the rule than the exception.

Jack and Jill

When I think of ADHD's social deficits, two of my former middle school students come to mind. Jack and Jill (not their

73

real names, obviously) are typical examples of how ADHD interferes with socially appropriate behavior. As far as peers were concerned, they were the kids to avoid.

Jill had a loud, squealing voice, was often heavy handed, and would fly off the emotional handle without warning. She cursed a lot. The other girls felt a little afraid of her. She had little sense of personal space. She would often touch another girl's hair. Without asking, she would take prized pencil boxes and jazzy pens to have a "look" at them. A lot of times she'd either drop or break what she touched.

Jill also had a hard time with "girl talk." She was an old pro at "motor mouth," which is expressive language, but she couldn't keep up with the speed or unspoken codes typical of girl talk. Her comments would be "off the wall" in relation to the subject. The girls called her "weird."

Jill had another typical ADHD problem. She couldn't see how or why she bugged others. That's because she was running on high motor and impulse, doing what struck her fancy from minute to minute in a highly charged, rapid-fire way.

Jack drove the entire school society up the wall, including the custodian who ran a youth fellowship and worked with all kinds of "problem kids." Jack did immature things, such as put his foot out when somebody walked by his desk. He'd say stuff that stung other kids. Similar to Jill, Jack couldn't see the effect his behavior had on himself or others.

Jack got his jollies from negative peer pressure. He'd alternate between class clown and school bully. Once he popped off at the mouth and threatened to "kill" a kid, which of course he didn't mean. Nonetheless, under the "no wiggle room, zero tolerance" policies strictly enforced in the wake of school shootings, Jack could not come back to school until he saw a psychiatrist.

One morning I asked Jack why he misbehaved. After a long pause, he said, "I'm not good at anything." We eventually stumbled upon something he did exceptionally well, which led to more positive behavior and acceptance by peers.

We can train social skills, but a kid such as Jack also needs to believe that he's got something of social value to trade. Find what your child does well (not necessarily exceptionally or perfectly). Use it as the cornerstone. Maybe it's running, biking, creating videos, or playing guitar. Maybe it is baseball, such as major league pitcher Scott Eyre talks about in his foreword to this book.

The Social Cost of Poor Self-Control

When minds drift, the connections between events tend to get lost. Kids with ADHD typically don't see the cause-and-effect relationship, whether we're talking about a social inter-action or figuring out how one thing led to another in a TV show plot. They miss key information. They can lose track of what's going on in a game, be disorganized, or get easily bored. It's not unusual for their minds to wander when they're supposed to keep their eye on the ball, or to interrupt, having missed a subtle social cue.

These children may lie to cover up an impulsive act. They often blame others, not because they do not have any character, but because they often don't see their role in events. Even when other children find their energy and spontaneity socially desirable, their peers' parents may not, which can create another avenue of social rejection.

A Lack of Empathy?

Children with ADHD often come across as unsympathetic to others' feelings and needs. They've been said to lack empathy, but I don't see this apparent insensitivity in the same light.

To be empathetic we have to understand how another feels without actually feeling those feelings. In essence, we're a few steps removed from the pain. I believe children with ADHD have trouble showing empathy because they have thin screens.

75

They feel too much, which triggers their reactivity. Seen in this light, perhaps we can understand their reactions and show them more empathy.

How Social Skills Are Learned

Most humans learn social skills this way: We observe, copy, and practice what we see others do. We take the feedback we get and either do more of what we do well or make adjustments. In a way, the learning seems intuitive. Children with ADHD do not learn this way. They generally don't pick up subtle social cues, so social skills must be taught in an obvious way: we have to use a system.

- ➲ Model.
- ➲ Copy.
- ➲ Practice.
- ➲ Feedback (especially positive attention).

For example, if you want to teach your child not to interrupt when you are on the phone, create a realistic "training" experience. First, explain the skill or goal, which in this case would be no interruptions. Discuss it and review potential reasons why he might interrupt. Then put it into action. When your child is on the phone, pretend you are about to interrupt and then say out loud what you would be thinking: "Oh, Tom's on the phone. I have to wait." Now, have your child copy the skill. Have someone call you and practice a few times. Give the child feedback every time he gets it right.

Using this formula will not guarantee that your child learns to use the skills he's been taught. Remember, so much of ADHD inappropriate behavior has to do with what researcher Russell Barkley terms "managed by the moment." Kids with ADHD may know a skill, but their impulsivity doesn't give them the wait time to call it forth and use it appropriately. Like all else that we do to manage ADHD, these kids will need to have a signal or gentle nudge that reminds them to do what they know. Don't let your child be "cueless." When you are training skills, let your child know what cues you'll use just in case.

You may have discovered what many parents of kids with ADHD know so well. As a parent, you can be a wonderful social skills model, but your child may not accept you as the social skills teacher. Children learn skills best when they are taught and reinforced in the setting where they are used. So, if your child has social problems at school, that's a good place to deal with the authentic issues. The same goes for issues at home. A treatment professional can be of great assistance here because one of your goals is to reduce parent/child conflict and negative feedback as much as possible.

> *When you find something that works for a certain situation, you have to make changes to it from time to time.*

Social Solutions

Following are some ideas to help with specific problems your child may experience. Understand that they may only work some of the time. An important understanding about ADHD management is this: When you find something that does work for a given situation, you have to make changes to it from time to time. Otherwise, it becomes too much of the same thing and, thus, boring. It loses stimulation value and won't hold your child's attention.

Inattention and Disinhibition

➲ Be active!

➲ Provide a lot of structure, supervision, and

rules, an adult nearby to step in as needed, and lots of positive attention).

⊃ Prepare for changes in routine.

⊃ Use nondirective play. (Do things that don't "teach" the child—such as shooting hoops, drawing, and so on. To build morale, let the child win in a nonobvious way.)

The Past Doesn't Guide the Present

⊃ Use a silent signal to guide social cues, such as one finger up for "wait."

⊃ Rehearse skill strategies, try to enter or leave a room, and practice greetings and social conversations.

⊃ Model and coach the use of strategies.

Mood Management

⊃ Keep it cool!

⊃ Have a "chill out" space.

⊃ Prepare when transitions are about to occur.

⊃ Cool, calm, collected—you and the environment.

Maintaining Relationships

⊃ Use social bridge-building.

⊃ Find a potential friend/play date.

⊃ Structure a time-limited, highly organized activity of mutual interest. Repeat the process and lengthen the time with each success.

Rejection and Isolation

- ➲ Build a social community.
- ➲ Find a mentor (perhaps an older child) to play with and be your child's "guiding" friend, especially someone who can help your child develop a special area of interest.
- ➲ Buddy up with a younger child who your child can mentor.
- ➲ Encourage volunteering (for neighbors, faith-based organizations, and community groups).

Many children who have social difficulties do well provided they have outlets and places where they can connect. Often these are places where they feel needed and worthwhile. Remember: it's not the number of people we can count as friends, but the quality of the friendships that counts. Your child can receive a lot from one good friend. Make that an initial goal.

Question 10

what's Happening to Our Family?

ADHD creates many challenges for a family, especially when hyperactivity and impulsivity are present. Because ADHD is a "hidden disability"—meaning children are born with it, but signs and symptoms may take years to pinpoint—the effects of the disorder can catch families off guard.

Parents tend to disagree over the best way to "discipline." Partners often become irritable, critical, and resentful of each other. Sibling conflicts tend to be more frequent and intense.

If your family seems "messed up," know that you are not alone. By the time of diagnosis, many families experience distress. It's important for family members to understand that it is ADHD and not the child with ADHD that creates the turmoil.

It's also important to know that ADHD is not the only stressor. Families are very complex systems. Family members bring personal characteristics and coping styles. Some of these tend to get along better with ADHD than others. For instance, family dynamics can be more complicated if one of the parents has ADHD, suffers from depression or other mental health issues, or is stress reactive.

When the System Is Out of Whack

Distressed families usually develop some dysfunctional patterns. Between ADHD problems, parental background, and family stressors, it's not surprising that our families often develop out-of-whack patterns of interaction. These get supported by subtle and powerful forces. You may recognize some of the following typical problems often found in our families.

Coalitions

Some coalitions can be helpful, especially if the two people joined together are Mom and Dad working for the well-being of the child. In dysfunctional systems, it's usually a parent and child who work against the other parent. Generally, this pattern does not occur because of deliberate intent, with one parent thinking, "Wow, I'll get on the kid's good side" or, "How can I undermine the other parent?" It's more subtle than that.

One parent is usually more lenient than the other. The child learns who to tool for what she wants. A parent starved for positive interaction with the child may unwittingly encourage this behavior. The parent who attempts to enforce discipline becomes the odd person out, which seriously undermines his or her ability to take charge. Over time, this pattern creates a very powerful child who plays one against the other. Marital conflict visits frequently. Some possible antidotes are:

- ➲ Present a united front.
- ➲ Disagree in private.
- ➲ Work as a team.
- ➲ Have rules and consequences you both agree on.

If you and your partner can't do these four bulleted items, seek professional help—ideally a clinician knowledgeable about ADHD's effects on family systems, as well as marriage and family issues. You would find such a person by asking resources you already have identified or by looking through the Yellow Pages in your local phone book. The therapist/client relationship is very important. Always screen any potential therapist before making a treatment commitment. Make sure she can work with both of you.

Triangles

In triangles, family members play the roles of the victim, the rescuer, and the villain. Generally, the child is the "victim." He or she misbehaves. The "villain" may attempt to punish the child for misbehavior, but the "rescuer" comes to the child's defense. That results in an alliance between the child and the rescuing parent. Of course, an alliance becomes a coalition over time. Some possible antidotes are:

➲ Understand that ADHD issues require guidance, not protection.

➲ Let your conscious mind, not your emotions guide you.

➲ Don't use the other parent as a way to feel better about yourself.

➲ Work as a team.

➲ Seek professional help.

The Scapegoat

Children with ADHD do not create all the family misery. Yet, often these kids feel like they do. Why? Well, they're similar to lightning rods that either send a charge up and down the family spine or wind up having Thor, the thunder god, come down on them with a loud bang for something they did or didn't do.

So, even though we may not actually intend to blame everything on the child with ADHD, they often perceive that we do. Either way, they feel like the scapegoat. Many times they unwittingly are. A new level of hostility often develops. You may find yourself with a very oppositional and defiant child. A few antidotes are:

➲ Catch the child being good—often.

➲ Reduce negative feedback.

➲ Create opportunities for shining moments.

Siblings and the Story of the "Too Good Child"

Many siblings don't get along. When ADHD is present, the opportunity for conflict grows larger, and the intensity of it goes deeper. Siblings of children with disabilities are often embarrassed by their brother's or sister's behavior. They worry others may see them as "bad," too. They get upset by the distress of their parents. Many feel frightened by their sibling with ADHD, who doesn't know his limits or boundaries. These siblings often see their prized personal possessions come to ruin.

> *Children with ADHD do not create all the family misery. Yet, often, these kids feel like they*

Siblings also tend to feel responsible and protective, isolated and out of the family loop, resentful, pressured to behave better and to excel at something, or guilt at not having the same struggles. Many show signs of extraordinary stress.

Some siblings become "white knights" or the "too good children" in an effort to bring family peace at any price. You might think, "Well, okay. At least these children gets a lot of positive feedback." That may be true, but being the "too good child" can also be the double-edged sword that sets an expectation for perfection that no child can live up to. It doesn't allow the siblings normal developmental opportunities to make and learn from mistakes. Finally, when there's a difficult child in a family, the best behavior of other children often goes ignored and unappreciated by overwhelmed parents making good behavior a somewhat devalued currency.

> *Some siblings become "white knights" or "too good children" in an effort to make peace.*

Do you know the saying "every dog gets its day?" That's what can happen with many siblings. They may become oppositional. Depending on the degree of family dysfunction, they may also develop substance problems, eating disorders, and depression. Some antidotes for this problem are:

- ➲ Share one-on-one time.
- ➲ Spend less time in whole family activities.
- ➲ Carefully structure family activities.
- ➲ Assign separate chores.
- ➲ Don't complain to other siblings about the ADHD child's behavior.
- ➲ Don't ask a sibling to pick up the slack.
- ➲ Teach problem-solving skills.

What's a Family to Do?

If your family has become lost in some of these unfortunate and potentially harmful patterns, conflict resolution skills can help you. Conflict resolution is a problem/solution driven approach that bypasses feelings and family dynamics in pursuit of a more reasoned way of handling issues. It combines effective communication skills with problem-solving methods.

The Road to Better Communication Skills

The road to better communication begins with recognition of how you presently communicate. Become mindful of what you say and how you say it. Listen to the words you use. Are they emotionally charged? Dramatic? Intended to evoke feelings of guilt or shame? Are they respectful? Chosen to limit emotionality? Do you grit your teeth? Do your eyes smile when you speak?

When your mode of communication changes, you'll eventually notice a difference in your child's style. Remember, change takes time. Old habits die hard. Being aware will certainly produce results. The following are additional guidelines:

- ➲ Let the speaker finish sentences.
- ➲ Concentrate on what is being said.
- ➲ Show interest with eye contact, facial expressions, and body language (when appropriate).
- ➲ Avoid judgments, put-downs, sarcasm, name-calling, and ridicule.
- ➲ Let the other person know when you agree.
- ➲ Praise the other person for using good skills.
- ➲ Monitor your tone of voice.
- ➲ Use active listening to be sure you understand what the other person is trying to communicate.

When listening actively, you respond by summarizing the speaker's main ideas and feelings and by showing appreciation for what she has to say—even if you disagree!

Here's an example of active listening: Support your child says, "I really hate my brother. He's so annoying and you always take his side. You should treat him like you treat me! Why does he get to stay up later than me?"

These statements are loaded with bait. If you bite, you'll be swallowed up in an argument. By actively listening, you might say, "I hear that you are upset about your brother and believe that you are not treated fairly. I appreciate what you have to say. Let's see what we can do about it."

At this point, you would move into basic problem-solving. Here's how.

Use a Problem-Solving Model

Problem-solving methods help to remove the emotion that lurks behind so many issues. Think of a problem as a weed. You see it, but often the cause is under the surface. To effectively solve a problem, you need to work on its cause and not its effect.

- ⤷ Identify the problem (be sure it's the root and not the branch).
- ⤷ Brainstorm possible solutions (don't automatically veto the wild and crazy).
- ⤷ Analyze and pick the most seemingly workable idea.
- ⤷ Evaluate the effects.
- ⤷ Try again if needed, or try another idea.

If your family's issues are not too severe, you can probably get these problem-solving and communication skills going on your own. Most families, however, generally need some type of professional help.

Let's go back to your child's issue, which she believes is "unfair" treatment. Identify the problem: Your child believes the treatment is unfair. This is where you would elaborate. Is the treatment unfair all the time, some of the time, or just on the bedtime issue? Be sure that you are solving the right problem. In this case, let's say the problem is that your child wants to stay up later and believes she should be able to because her brother does. Don't cloud the issue. Talking about the brother is a no-win situation. Stick to her problem—she wants to stay up as late as her brother.

Brainstorm possible solutions. Here is where you could list as many ideas as you and your child could come up with. Don't veto the wild and crazy. Some ideas you could try: include staying up later on weekends, earning the right to stay up later by doing all homework assignments on time, and staying up a half hour later for two weeks and see how it affects waking up and mood. If it's okay, then you can try adding 15 minutes more. Also, if she stays up as late as her brother, then she would have to get up at the same time he did.

Analyze the ideas and try the one that seems most likely to succeed. Evaluate how the solution worked. In this case, she got an extra half hour, which is still not the same as her brother's bedtime, but a workable compromise. Try something else if this solution doesn't pan out.

Divorce Matters

Children with ADHD do not cause divorce. ADHD stresses a marriage, but divorces occur for many reasons, mainly having to do with the way the couples relate to one another. Many feel contempt or hostility for each other. Interests and feelings change. They cannot see eye to eye on most things. Perhaps they were not committed in the first place. Maybe all of these apply. No matter what the reason, children with ADHD, who are so often in the middle of conflict, often feel they've caused a breakup. They need to know that they do not create or own responsibility for adult issues.

If you are getting a divorced or are already divorced, be sure to get counseling so that your child doesn't become an unintended casualty.

Question 11

when Is It ADHD and when Is It Misbehaving?

The question of whether misbehavior is due to ADHD or just plain old misbehavior leads me to think about which came first, the chicken or the egg. There's really no way to know. Every child misbehaves. Because ADHD is a behavioral disorder, expect that your child will misbehave more. Expect that your child will not readily learn from her mistakes or your efforts to correct misbehavior. Also, expect some people to accuse you or your child of using ADHD as an excuse. To these people, you may simply say, "Which came first? The chicken or the egg?"

Is ADHD Just an Excuse?

No, ADHD is not just an excuse. In fact, it's very important to be mindful that ADHD makes it much harder for your child to behave. This awareness allows you to make meaningful changes to the way you handle the behavioral problems. Meaningful change usually begins with altering beliefs and perceptions that can be so powerful that they interfere with the way you help your child. Think about the difference between these two sentences: My child *is* a behavior problem. My child *has* a behavior problem.

Though *is* and *has* are two small words, they are oceans apart in translation. The child who *has* a behavioral disorder does not deliberately choose to misbehave but does so anyway. "Has a behavioral problem" means it is reasonable to expect more behavioral mistakes more frequently than children without this disability.

There's another compelling reason to be mindful of ADHD when considering your child's behavior. When problems are viewed as being rooted in the child's disability rather than his personality, we're kinder. We tend to be less emotional. We seek solutions. We rise to the occasion! We use less punishment and blame. That does not mean we don't hold the child accountable for misbehavior. It just means that we do more to help the child help himself. We put a lot more effort into prevention and intervention rather than punishment.

> *Your child needs help to improve any behavior that creates problems.*

Enable, Don't Disable

In an earlier section, you read these words: your biology is not your biography. When it comes to misbehavior and ADHD, that statement is not entirely true. Just as a weakened immune system makes any of us more susceptible to viruses and infections, the biology of ADHD makes your child more susceptible to misbehaving. Thus, your child's story will have much more misbehavior in it.

Regardless of the root, your child needs help to improve any behavior that creates problems. To excuse misbehavior because of ADHD is enabling your child to be disabled. Remember, all that we do in the name of ADHD management has this primary purpose: to help normalize the child's behavior so that she can reduce negative effects and live a well-adjusted life.

This issue became so apparent to me when I was giving a workshop at a parenting conference. A mother who had enough with calls from the school about her ADHD son said, "He has ADHD. He can't help his behavior and I think they should get off his back. What do you think?"

I think a lot of misbehavior with ADHD happens because we don't do enough to create situations where problems are headed off before they come to a head. That's a parent's or teacher's skill issue—not a reason to place blame. In this case I said, "Is the problem that your child cannot follow the rules, or is the problem that there is no structure and support to help your child follow the rules?"

3 Steps to Improve Performance

There are three essential conditions that help kids with ADHD improve their performance.

1. Create a structure that helps him guide his behavior with rules and routines. For example, with academics, the structure would be tasks matched to his skill level so that it does not drive him to frustration.

2. Provide frequent positive feedback about how he is doing. Pay positive attention to any behaviors or approximations that are done well. Reward progress, not perfection. Redirect him when behavior goes off the mark.

3. Give consequences that are consistently linked to how he behaves. You will want to know what these are ahead of time, and so will he. (Behavior charts, covered in Question 14, are a great way to do this.)

These three conditions apply to behavioral, academic, and social performance. Once you master the art of creating these conditions, you simply reproduce them on large and small scales to guide and assist your child.

For example, you want to get your child to the dinner table on time.

Structure: Dinner is served at roughly the same time every night, which creates a routine.

Rule: You must be seated at the table before the food is served. You might give your child the chore of setting the table so she is in the vicinity of the table when the food is served. This also provides your child with another opportunity to earn privileges for doing chores.

Frequent Feedback: You monitor whether or not your child is there on time (or if you have to give "reminders," and how many). By the way, you should never give more than one reminder unless you also give a negative consequence for needing to issue a second reminder. Praise your child when she's there on time.

Consequences: The praise you give in the feedback stage would be the consequence of doing what is expected. But you could sweeten the pie by charting her performance over a seven-day period and making a special reward, such as dinner out at a restaurant or picking the meals for the next two days.

Common Misbehaviors—What to Do

Why are certain misbehaviors more common, more frequent, and more resistant to correction? Each of the three ADHD core symptoms undermines the brain's ability to regulate itself consistently. Perhaps you recognize some or all of the following comments typically made by children with ADHD about their misbehavior.

"I'll Never Do It Again!"

There's a reason the best intentions of your child often go astray. Those of us without ADHD learn from our experiences. We say, "Hey, the last time I ran through the living room, I tripped on the rug and hit my head on the coffee table. I'm not gonna do that again." With ADHD, the past doesn't guide the decision-making of the present.

As researcher Russell Barkley says, "ADHD is not a problem of knowing what to do. It's a problem of doing what you know." Even when kids with ADHD learn from their mistakes, they often don't have the wherewithal to let the learning guide the present action. This shows up as noncompliance with rules, risktaking types of behavior, knowing better but doing it anyway, carelessness, difficulty following instructions, and delaying gratification.

What to Do:

Here's a great place to use the three steps to improve performance, as was previously described. Follow the three steps for every house rule.

- ➲ Make house rules (no more than five).
- ➲ Post the house rules where they can be readily seen.
- ➲ Give frequent positive feedback.
- ➲ Give prompts and reminders about behavior and rules.
- ➲ Have preset consequences.

In addition to using the three steps, you'll also want to teach your child how to correct his behavior. The following two methods will help you with that.

Learn how to use STAR: Stop, Think, Act, Respond. This method is very easy. Teach it to your child, then practice using it. Here's how: When your child is about to misbehave or is in the midst of inappropriate behavior, say "STAR" and hold up your hand with your fingers spread out similar to a starfish. Until your child learns what this word means and can recite it at any time, you then say, "Stop. Think. What should you be doing? Act. Respond. Nice correction. Good job."

Use mild correction. This might be a time-out; a loss of a privilege; or a statement that speaks to the behavior, such as "Stop. That behavior is not acceptable" rather than "I expect better behavior from you!"

This Is Boring!!!

We all have different levels of interest. Let's face it. Some tasks are more boring than others. So why do many kids without ADHD stick with boring tasks and finish? Why doesn't your kid do the same regardless of whether or not she has a point about the dullness of the task? It's biology. A key neurological problem of ADHD is not enough stimulation to sustain attention.

Typically, when faced with a boring task, your child may be driven to cut corners; not finish tasks and chores; or do things to stimulate interest, such as take apart telephones, reprogram computers, throw objects at windows to hear the sound, and so on.

What to Do:

- ⊃ Make chores more interesting and attractive.
- ⊃ Limit amount of time spent on "boring" activities.
- ⊃ Alternate boring tasks with interesting tasks.
- ⊃ Avoid unnecessary repetition.

For example, if your child resists or avoids cleaning her bedroom, break the job down into small parts. Figure out how many minutes she can stay with this task. Then tell your child that she can spend no more than a certain amount of time doing that task. Decide which area(s) of the room will be cleaned during that time. Be clear about what the final product standard is. Set a timer and leave. (Don't hang in the doorway and hawk out commands and directions. That is a guaranteed way to get a mutiny going. Promise a surprise when time is up and the job has met the agreed upon standards. (Don't go in there and redo the job because its not perfect. Begin with a lower standard.)

Look at the previous bulleted list and determine which principles were shown in this example. Whenever you need to deal with a "boring" situation, whether it's homework, other chores, or whatever, problem-solve and apply these bulleted principles to your solution.

Oh! Was I Supposed to Do That?

If you don't have ADHD and want to know what it's like to not have enough attention, try this experiment. Call someone, check your e-mail, and pay a bill by check all at the same time. How'd you do? Miss any details? Make any mistakes?

In today's world, we like to think that we multitask. We don't. The human brain cannot sustain attention to two things at once. What it can and does do is rapidly shift from one point of focus to another, and then rapidly shift back when and if appropriate. What appears to be multitasking is actually the brain's attention network operating at high speed.

With ADHD, once attention is diverted, it is more likely to continue to wander in search of interesting things. That is why kids with ADHD generally need to have their attention redirected by some external source. Think of the sustained attention problem of ADHD as a car that constantly slips out of gear and can only get back into drive with the help of an external gear shift.

"Not enough attention" means forgetfulness, missing details (often the important ones), wandering from tasks, disorganization, incompletion, in one ear and out the other, and difficulty following through on instructions.

What to Do:

- ➲ Have schedules and organizational routines.
- ➲ Make important details stand out.
- ➲ Use lists, checklists, and reminders.
- ➲ Break tasks into smaller parts.
- ➲ Make chores interesting and rewarding.
- ➲ Add stimulation to the dull things.
- ➲ Give some motor activity.

There's no magic here—just set up work that pays off and eventually takes you less time. By helping your child with these external prompts and monitoring devices, you accomplish two parts of the three-step "improve performance" method: structure and feedback. Checklists and reminders provide feedback. Of course, always use the third part of this method and give consequences—positive or negative. If you find yourself giving too many negative consequences, analyze the situation. Chances are there's a flaw in the structure that needs to be tweaked. Question 13 goes into detail about rules and consequences.

I Don't Mean to Be in Your Face!

Where self-control is concerned, having too little often means having too much behavior somewhere else. Poor self-control often masks as immaturity, rudeness, and messiness. Your child may talk too much, too loudly, and make it hard for anyone else to get a word in edgewise. The tendency to reach out and touch everything often leads to broken pieces. Understand that lack of self-control is not a moral issue it. It's not about willpower. It's about having enough biochemical oomph to get started, get going, and run smoothly.

What to Do:
- ➲ Provide a lot of structure.
- ➲ Have routines and schedules.
- ➲ Signal upcoming transitions.
- ➲ Speak in a calm, quiet voice.
- ➲ Alternate stimulating with quieting activities.
- ➲ Provide a cue to use STAR method—Stop, Think, Act, Respond.

> *Where self-control is concerned, having too little often means having too much of a different behavior.*

Does Anybody Really Know What Time It Is?

Time. There's never enough and always too much, particularly when you have ADHD. Your child may not have a good sense of time or timing. For some reason, the internal clock doesn't seem to work too efficiently. If you have ADHD and self-management does not come easily, you can expect to be untimely, not only in the completion of tasks, but also in the entrance or exit to social situations.

What to Do:
- ➲ Use a daily schedule.
- ➲ Practice time estimation skills.
- ➲ Reward on-time performance.

⊃ Use external signals for inappropriate and appropriate timing.

⊃ Use timers and watches.

There are a number of devices that help with time management. Web search using the keywords "ADHD time management tools." Think in terms of clocks, timers, sport watches with timers or vibrators (although these can be disruptive in classrooms), and so on.

To practice time estimation skills, develop a game with your child. Each of you guesses how long a specific task will take, for example, taking out the garbage. Time it and then have a prize for the winner. Resist the temptation to link the prize to something unpleasant (For example, "If I (Mom or Dad) win, you have to take out the garbage for the rest of your life.

Gotta Have It Now

Most children with ADHD hate to wait! The circumstances don't seem to matter, either. Research shows that when promised a much greater reward for delaying gratification, our children will opt for the smaller reward just to get it now!

What to Do:

⊃ Avoid places that have "wait" times (restaurants, store lines and so on).

⊃ Give them something active to do while waiting, such as a puzzle, video game, or music.

⊃ Don't make the future too far off! Think and plan in terms of the "foreseeable" future. If you promise something that's too far off, you will get nagged to death!

Routine Resistance

Does your child have trouble with bedtime, mealtime, and getting dressed or undressed? What may seem like a simple routine to you or me is not all that easy for the brain that has trouble shifting attention and energy, especially to a task that isn't all that interesting or rewarding.

What to Do:

- ➲ Have the same daily schedule.
- ➲ Reward for on-time performance.
- ➲ Do a quieting activity before bothersome routine.
- ➲ Use praise and positive feedback.
- ➲ Have a bedtime ritual, perhaps preparation for the next day.
- ➲ Limit the duration of mealtimes and other routines.

> *Remember, you have to manage ADHD to make ADHD manageable.*

Intentional or Accidental Behavior?

Sometimes kids do intentionally choose to misbehave. And sometimes they lack experience to know better. Kids with ADHD have these problems plus the added issues that come with the disorder. Some children with ADHD may act as if they don't want to get with the program as a defense mechanism for not being readily able to do so. You have to know that, in their hearts, they want to please and do well.

Don't get hung up on whether behavior is intentional or accidental. Be a take-charge parent. Identify problems. Seek solutions.

Q*uestion* 12

Am I Doing Something Wrong?

Wouldn't parenting be so much easier if there were a rule book with no exceptions? Unfortunately, there are no parenting rules—no words of wisdom you can apply at all times to all situations. Still, we do have great guidelines. When ADHD is present, we parents tend to spend a lot of time living with the exception to the great guidelines. We do what we think will work to raise well-behaved, happy, well-adjusted children who one day will become competent, happy, loving, well-adjusted adults.

Ahhhh! As far as I can recall, there isn't even a fairy tale that has this story line, but somehow many of us buy into the myth that our children will live "happily ever after because I did a good job of raising them." ADHD exposes the fault lines and stress fractures in any system.

Losing Unrealistic Expectations

One of the graces ADHD sends is the "get realistic" grace. It guides us to get rid of ridiculous expectations and beliefs.

We are not bad or good parents. We are simply parents doing the best we can to raise exceptional children. Unfortunately, we tend to pick up some pretty ineffective parenting techniques that lead us to ask, "Am I doing something wrong?"

Not really. Many of the parenting techniques we use for our children with ADHD work pretty well for children without the disorder. But ADHD exposes the fault lines and stress fractures in any system. Until we learn to identify the practices that don't serve our intentions or our children very well, the home scene can become a battleground. Often the seeds of this conflict begin with some irrational beliefs.

> *Often the seeds of conflict begin with some irrational beliefs.*

What Do You Believe?

Psychologist Arthur Robin identified a set of beliefs that parents typically have that lead them into conflict, especially with their adolescents. Maybe I was ahead of the curve (maybe you are too) because I certainly found these irrational beliefs swarming in my head while my children were still quite young.

Until I could expose these beliefs to the clear light of day, they would continue to undermine my parenting decisions and my ability to respond in a thoughtful, mindful way using effective practices that you'll read about in the next chapter.

Look over the following list. If you buy into any of these irrational beliefs, write them down as little notes. Either before, during, or after any conflict with your child, look at your notes. Immediately acknowledge the irrational beliefs and convert to reasonable expectations, such as the following examples give.

Ruination

Irrational Belief: Whatever my child's doing or not doing will lead to the ruination of her life. No good will come from this. This is the last straw.

Reasonable Expectation: This too shall pass. This is just a moment in time—a single event. We can do damage control.

Obedience

Irrational Belief: He should do what he is told. He's not going to get away with this. There are no ifs, ands, or buts.

Reasonable Expectation: All kids misbehave from time to time. Whether intended or not, it's a behavioral mistake, not a moral flaw. Mistakes have consequences. The consequence will be in proportion to the misdeed.

Perfectionism

Irrational Belief: She didn't do what she was supposed to do. She lost yet another pair of shoes. My child is old enough to do better.

Reasonable Expectation: I guess I have to expect less and be more involved. I have to help my daughter structure time and tasks. We need to figure out how to help my daughter keep track of her shoes.

Malicious Intent

Irrational Belief: My kid is deliberately trying to drive me crazy. He knows I hate it when he does that but he does it anyway! He's provoking another fight on purpose. I'll show him who's boss!

Reasonable Expectation: I know ADHD makes it harder for my child to behave. I won't take this personally. Instead, I'll take a deep breath, go back to the rules and consequences, and use them accordingly.

Love/Appreciation

Irrational Belief: I spent all my extra cash on the new bike for him and he left it out in the rain. My child never thinks of anyone but himself.

Reasonable Expectation: This is not a reflection of my child's love and affection or a hate crime! Guess she'll have to learn from this mistake and do without the bike for a few days.

What Does Your Child Believe?

Dr. Robin notes that your children, especially adolescents, have unreasonable beliefs, too. Similar to parents, they think your interventions are unfair and will lead to the ruination of their lives. They also will confuse your discipline efforts as a lack of your love and appreciation. (On the lack of appreciation, note that they may be right! Kids with ADHD tend to get so much negative feedback that their good deeds often go unnoticed.)

Ineffective Parenting Practices

The idea behind behavioral change is to recognize patterns that don't work and replace them with more effective patterns. Awareness is the first step toward change. You don't have to do anything right now except become mindful of when you slip into these patterns.

- **No action plan:** No explicitly stated rules and no pre-agreed-upon consequences so that the child knows what to do and what to expect.

- **Too much negativity:** An abundance of negative feedback packaged in many forms, with a focus on what's been done wrong.

- **Too little positive feedback:** Doing what is expected yields little or no positive benefit. It's an expectation rather than an appreciation.

➲ **Distorted perceptions:** In addition to the beliefs mentioned previously, certain words are used to describe misbehavior, including *always, never, should,* and *could.* For instance, do you ever say, "My kid is always angry"?

➲ **Inconsistent consequences:** The same misbehavior is dealt with differently, depending on your mood or the way you're feeling. Sometimes you might actually be amused by a behavior that drove you crazy the day before. For example, your child is making loud noises. You are on the phone with a relative and you have them listen in to the noises because they are funny and entertaining. The next day, you are on the phone with your boss, and your child does the same thing. Only this time, you yell at him for making bird calls. Mixed messages make for mixed-up kids.

➲ **Noncontingent punishment:** The child gets punished or blamed for things he didn't do, especially when he is given the scapegoat role. For example, you are still irked about something from the day before and today you fly off the handle because your child leaves stuff around, even though you have a preset schedule for when stuff is to be picked up.

➲ **Good cop/bad cop:** You and the other parent have a routine going where one of you takes a kind, gentle approach and the other plays ogre. Translation: "Wait until your father (mother) gets home!"

➲ **What did you say?:** Parents of children with ADHD, especially mothers who are naturally verbal, tend to use more words than necessary with their kids in an effort to get them to comply. In other words, you may train your child not to listen to you.

➲ **All talk/no action:** You become the ultimate bag of hot air, asking, pleading, cajoling, and talking but never delivering consequences.

103

⊃   **Talk/reason:** You try to convince the child about why she should behave, usually with the carrot being something far off in the future that does not impress your child in the least, such as "study hard now so you can go to a great college" or "Eat your broccoli because you want to have strong bones and healthy teeth so that when you are as old as your grandparents you won't have to wear dentures." Children with ADHD respond to action and consequences, not reasoning. They are the "do it now" kids, so don't give reasons—give results!

⊃   **Warnings, more warnings, and threats:** Your warnings, especially when seldom or haphazardly followed through with the consequences you've promised, teach your child that you don't mean what you say and she should push the envelope. The more you say, the more you are ignored, and the more likely the interactions will grow in hostility.

⊃   **Tit for tat:** Researchers at the University of Massachusetts found that some parents developed a very immature style in which they reacted to their child's behavior in a "you get what you give" type of response. The problem here, of course, is adults need to be governed by reason not reaction.

⊃   **Russian roulette:** Unpredictable and harsh, in this type of response, you basically have a parent who gives a lot of threats, and never follows through, until that one time when the gun goes off, and the kid takes a hit—often for something minor. It's a harsh and extreme reaction, and it does not teach or discipline the child. It trains fear instead.

⊃   **Forget about it!:** This parent is either tired out from all of the previous examples and just says, "It's no big deal anyway. I might as well not get all upset."

Or the parent wants to be thought of as "nice" or "a good friend," or "wants to win the child's love." Either way, no consequences spells trouble. Expect all hell to break lose.

Power Problems

Most parent/child power plays are not preplanned strategic events. They're land mines that get tripped accidentally, especially when our parenting practices look an awful lot like those just described. Why?

A possible reason has to do with leadership. When children lose confidence in the leadership, they tend to take matters into their own hands in an attempt to feel safe and in control. This attempt to seize power is generally not driven by conscious thought. It's emotional, limbic, and knee-jerk reactive. It's trouble with a capital T!

Families engaged in power struggles fall into abusive, reactive patterns. Expect to hear a lot of name-calling, sarcasm, yelling, and screaming. Expect humiliation. Expect hitting of people or things, or throwing and breaking of stuff in angry fits. Expect these behaviors from both parent and child.

Manipulation

Ineffective parenting practices may also teach your child to play your emotional strings to get what she wants. Kids do try to withhold their love and approval. If you take this bait and give in to your kid to win their acceptance and love, you have unwittingly given your child a lot of power. For instance, suppose your child withholds a bedtime kiss in order to delay lights out and to continue to get your attention. Giving in to get that one final kiss almost guarantees a repeat performance the following night. Over time, you may have a nightmare on your hands. As the cliché goes, be a parent, not your child's friend.

Oppositional Defiant Disorder (ODD)

ODD tends to show up in families where there are a lot of ineffective parenting practices going on, particularly ones that are highly reactive and driven by emotion. Is ODD something a child's predisposed to based on biology? Do parents cause ODD, or does ODD cause parents to be more reactive? There's no way to know these answers. Don't get caught up in the chicken/egg riddle.

What we do know is that kids with ODD need to have parents who use very intentional, thoughtful, effective, and positive practices. Few parents come by these skills naturally. You will most likely need professional help to dig out of an ODD mess.

As a side note, I hate the term "ODD." It has too many negative connotations and sounds like "demon" or "monster." Similar to children with ADHD, children with ODD are *in* trouble, not the *cause* of trouble. We need this perceptual change to alter the way we respond to these children.

We also need to take care of what we say in front of an ADHD child. I've heard many parents and clinicians refer to a child as "ODD." I've heard parents go into great detail about their kid's ODD and "rotten" behavior within the child's earshot. Stop and think! Imagine what seeds are planted in the child's mind! Defiance worsens when children feel badly about themselves. We want to show troubled children redemption, not condemnation. Look for the positive. Build on it. Be mindful of your words.

Question 13

What Parenting Practices Work Best?

Do you sometimes wonder if there's a magic parenting book no one's told you about? There's not, but there are practices and parenting styles that seem to work magic with ADHD.

Researchers find that children with ADHD behave better for parents who might be described as follows:

They are both loving and firm. They generously give praise and appreciation. They believe rules are important, but don't mind explaining the rules or involving their child in their creation. They are clear about the rules, intentionally flexible about them at times, but do not negotiate rules created for issues of safety. They use consequences, and show appreciation when the child behaves. Basically, they are cool, calm, collected, consistent, and creative.

Positive Parenting Practices

Catch the Child Being Good

The best way to encourage behavior is to pay attention to it! Kids with ADHD can and often do behave appropriately,

107

but many good deeds go unnoticed or unacknowledged. If you don't pay positive attention to your child's positive behavior, then he won't really be taught about what's appropriate and what is not. Where other kids may come by this knowledge just by observing and connecting the dots, the attention and self-control issues of ADHD often cause your child to miss such important details. You don't want your child to get it right by accident. These are the children who need clear guidelines, constant feedback, and positive reinforcement.

The Art of Being Positive

Pretend this book is a supersize scribble pad. Right now, use bright green markers. Jot down everything that comes to mind about how to catch your child being good and how to give positive feedback. Not sure this is necessary? Try this little experiment.

Carry a piece of paper for a day and draw a smiley face every time you pay positive attention to your child. Tomorrow, consciously double the smiles. Keep doubling the smiles until you see that at least 80 percent of the interactions with your child are positive. Ask yourself: Are we happier? Is there more peace in our home?

Not sure how to pay positive attention? Here are some ideas to get you started:

- ➲ Say, "Good job!" "I love you." "You're doing great." "I'm proud of you."
- ➲ Send a cheery e-mail!
- ➲ Smile when you see your child.
- ➲ Say "hello."
- ➲ Play a game your child's good at!
- ➲ Point out what was done well, even if the goal was not met.

Rules and Consequences to Live By

Rules help all of us modify our behavior, especially when we know the consequences. For instance, we all know speeding can result in a ticket. Many of us follow speed limits not only because we might get a ticket, but also because we respect the safety factors and want to avoid the consequences of unsafe driving. Safety alone should be enough reason to follow the limit. So why do some of us still push the pedal?

We don't hold the consequences in mind, especially without external reminders. We get away with breaking the rule more often than not, meaning we don't have accidents every time we speed. Yet speeders usually slow down on stretches of road the police frequent. Why? There's a clear and present consequence just waiting. We tell ourselves, "Slow down."

ADHD is very much a disorder where internal monologues to guide behavior are absent. Rules and their consequences need to be externalized. You need patrol cars along the way as reminders. When you make a rule, you need to enforce the rule. Because we want to encourage and train the development of appropriate behavior, we don't want to emphasize the penalty driven "got cha" consequences. We want to give positive feedback whenever the child follows the rules.

> *ADHD is a disorder where internal monologues to guide behavior are absent.*

Rule-Making Guidelines

1. Have a family meeting and get input from all members about what rules are needed.

2. State the rules in terms of what behavior you want instead of what you don't want. For example, "go to bed on time" rather than "do not put off bedtime."

3. Have a list of consequences for following the rules.

4. Consequences can be either logical or natural—positive or negative. Logical consequences are those you create that have something to do with the situation. For instance, a smile and "thank you" for putting toys away.

Natural consequences are those that happen without you having to do anything. For instance, toys left outside in the rain will be rusted and no longer of use. You can add a logical consequence to a natural one: "The toys are ruined naturally, and logically will not be replaced by you." Beware of overkill.

Consequences need to have "market" value for your child. If a situation arises where you don't have a preplanned consequence, learn to say, "I'm going to think about this first and then take action." If you delay, be sure you do return to the issue.

5. Reinforce the rules consistently—even when you're tired and don't feel like it!

6. Post the rules so everyone can see them.

7. Have all children follow the rules—and parents, too, where appropriate.

8. Use intentional flexibility. There may be times you want to change or alter a rule.

Sample rules: Create rules you can and want to live by. For example:

- ⊃ Treat all family members with respect, including pets.
- ⊃ Go to bed on time.
- ⊃ Eat dinner on time.
- ⊃ Walk in the house, don't run.
- ⊃ Use an inside voice when inside.
- ⊃ Clean up after yourself.

Sample Consequences: Create consequences that are reasonable, related, and respectful. For example:

➲ Positive attention, especially praise.

➲ Special treat for catching self in the act and modifying behavior.

➲ Dessert.

➲ Extra time in a rewarding activity.

Time Out or Chill Out

When kids have trouble behaving or get in an emotional state that's bound to lead them down the path of no return, time out can be a very effective intervention when used correctly. Time out literally means taking time away from a situation to defuse emotionality and give the child (or adult) time to make a mental reset in order to get with the program. Don't threaten time out. It's not a punishment, its a cool down.

➲ Have a predesignated, quiet, low-stimulation place.

➲ Have a predetermined length of time to be there (usually one minute equaling the age of the child. (For example, if he's nine years old, then nine minutes).

➲ Set a timer.

➲ Repeat as necessary.

Your child may balk or resist. That's because he is in an emotionally charged state. Stick to your command and keep your cool. If your child goes but leaves early, simply return your child to time out until he completes it. You may have to be consistent like this for a couple of weeks until your child gets the message. Eventually, your child will see this as restorative and not punitive. Some children have even been known to put themselves in time out!

111

Effective Commands

One surefire way to wind up in a parent/child mess is to be ineffective in the way you give commands. There's an art to getting a child to do what you want, especially if that child has ADHD. For some reason, kids with ADHD tend to listen more to their fathers than their mothers. To understand this paternal art and where a mother's paint gets thick and drippy or why her brush strokes miss the mark, let's look at a typical scenario.

Generally, when fathers want something done, they don't say, "Hi Sweetie, would you mind taking out the garbage? I really need this done because if we don't take out the garbage, we'll be living in a garbage dump, and it might smell bad, and the neighbors might complain, and the Board of Health might not let us live here anymore...." And before Mom knows it, her child has either left the room or is asking a million questions about the Board of Health and where they would live if they got kicked out. Then Dad comes home and says, "Take the garbage out." And it gets canned! And the difference between Mom and Dad is...?

How to Give Commands

➲ Have your child's attention before you give a command. (Try not to interrupt a highly rewarding activity.)

➲ Make a direct, positive request, not a "would you please" question.

➲ Give one command at a time.

➲ Use emotional control—a soft but firm voice.

➲ Give commands that you can easily watch your child do.

➲ Give feedback for compliance—immediate, frequent, and enthusiastic.

➲ Avoid nagging, warnings, and threats. Its do or don't do.

112

➲ Give time for the child to obey—3 to 5 seconds. (Here's where many of us fall apart. We don't give the child time to shift the mental set from what they are doing to what needs to be done. We immediately start giving more commands. Our emotional tone rises as we feel ignored. The kid becomes reactive. Pretty soon, the focus is off the command and on to a battle.)

When Your Child Doesn't Comply

If your child doesn't seem to be able to follow your commands, there are some possible reasons you need to explore. Does your child:

1. Understand the requirements? (Be specific. Practice.)

2. Understand what is appropriate? (Review rules.)

3. Have the skills to do what is asked? (Train in steps and approximations.)

4. Need to be coached in every situation? (Guide, don't nag.)

5. Do "good enough" performance? (Be happy with compliance even if it comes with moans and groans. Reinforce attempts to comply.)

Training Response-ability

I'm a great believer in clueing people in about why I'm doing certain things, especially children who might not get the rationale on their own. Here's a simple model used by many people to help children take responsibility for their behavior. Before you use this approach, explain it to your child.

3 Seconds to "Stop and Think"

➲ Give a command.

➲ Wait three seconds. If the command is not followed, put your coach hat on. Say:

113

- ⟳ Stop and Think. (Wait three seconds.)
- ⟳ Are you going to make a good choice/or bad choice? (Wait three seconds.)
- ⟳ Do you know what the choices are and what steps are needed? (Wait three seconds.)
- ⟳ Just do it! (Wait three seconds.)
- ⟳ If it's done, don't wait three seconds.
- ⟳ Give immediate positive feedback. Then ask: "How did that work out for you?"

Stop and Think falls under the category of cognitive behavioral training. It makes behavior a clear choice. It focuses on your child's actions. It's a safety net so you don't fall into the nagging, screaming, pulling-your-hair-out pattern. The three seconds gives your child time to process.

Most kids with ADHD will not readily use these techniques without some type of external guide leading the way. That doesn't mean it isn't working. It just means that ADHD requires more "hands on." "Stop and think" is a way to be "hands on" without hitting!

You have to practice. Positive discipline is an art. Don't be hard on yourself for mistakes. Simply return to the drawing board. You may find you need art lessons as many parents do. I highly encourage parent training. Your child's pediatrician should know where you can get this help.

Question 14

?

Does My Child Need a Behavior Chart?

Your child may have certain chronic behavior problems that might be helped by using a behavior chart. A behavior chart is similar to a daily report card. First, you select a few of your child's problem behaviors; for example, not following rules, not doing what is asked, or not getting ready on time for school. You put these on a chart. Each day, your child receives points or tokens that can be exchanged for rewards and privileges. When designed and used properly, behavior charts work very well.

Behavior Basics

There's a sample chart in this chapter. Before creating one for your child, you'll want to know why you are doing what you are doing. Let's look at some basic behavior management principles, beginning with my big mess up!

How I Turned My Dog Into a Cracker Addict

Mollie didn't bark. She howled. When I first got her, a friend told me that when I let her out to "do her business" I should encourage her to come back by giving her a dog cracker. Made good sense to me!

Mollie would go out, do her business, and then howl as she ran up to me. I'd hold the cracker out. She'd howl again. I'd give her a cracker, thinking it was a reward for coming back. What did I really do? *I accidentally rewarded undesirable behavior.* I trained her to howl for crackers. Before long, she had a two-box-a-week habit. Mollie actually learned to howl when I was on the phone, knowing that I would give her a cracker just to quiet her. Does this sound familiar?

What I Needed to Know

Behavior scientists talk about behavior as an ABC equation:

(A) Something happens that sets the stage for a behavior to occur. That's an antecedent.

(B) The behavior happens.

(C) A consequence follows. The consequence either encourages or discourages the behavior from recurring.

Mollie's behavior was to howl for crackers. The antecedent was my giving her a cracker every time she howled. The consequence of her howling was my rewarding her with a cracker. If I had realized my mistake early on, it would have been much easier for me to break her of this habit. Alas, I didn't. In this case the antecedent became the consequence.

Important Behavior Principles

The best way to increase a behavior is to pay attention to it. To discourage behavior, ignore it (if at all possible). Teach replacement behavior. For instance, I could have trained Mollie to "play dead" instead of howl. Talk about peace and quiet!

What Pets and Parents Have in Common

All behavior, whether it's "good" or "bad," has a purpose. We want to get something, get away from something, or avoid something. Mollie wanted a cracker. Why did she howl? Though unintentional, I trained her. Do you accidentally reward behavior with attention—positive or negative?

Behavior management has two guiding rules:

1. Reward desirable behavior.
2. Don't accidentally reward undesirable behavior.

Parents and pet owners commonly make these mistakes:

1. Accidentally reward undesirable behavior.
2. Don't reward desirable behavior. (We may even punish good behavior. For instance, your child says, "Excuse me" to interrupt, and you yell, "Not now." What does your child learn? If I want to be heard, best to skip formalities. I have to spit it out loud and fast.

How Charts Help

Behavior charts allow you to focus on routinely occurring behaviors that you want your child to change. Attention is the most powerful of all rewards. Charts train you to pay positive attention to behavior you are trying to encourage. They guide you to reward desirable behavior or withhold rewards when your child doesn't meet a behavioral expectation. This way, your child is accountable to herself for what she did or did not do. Charts help both you and your child track and monitor behavior in a concrete, focused, and highly visible way.

How to Make a Chart

You will need a piece of paper (doesn't have to be fancy); either poker chips, points, or stars to give to your child whenever he does the desirable behavior; and a list of rewards your child can exchange for earnings.

Here's what you do:

1. Make a list of behaviors you want to encourage. (No more than three to five, depending on your child's age. When your child masters a desired behavior, replace it with another one that needs work.)

2. State the behaviors in positive terms. (For example, picks up toys" instead of "doesn't leave toys around.")

3. Be on the lookout to catch the child doing the behavior.

4. Whenever you notice the behavior, give your child a chip, point, or put a star on the chart.

5. Every night, tally the day's earnings.

6. Allow your child to exchange earnings for rewards which can be:

   A. Activities (play a game with you, for example).

   B.Privileges (special or routinely occurring such as watching TV).

   C.Social rewards (have a sleepover, shoot hoops with you, and so on).

Similar to a store, stock up with a list of rewards that you and your child create ahead of time. Each "stock" item costs a certain amount of chips, points, or stars. "Price" rewards according to their reinforcement value.

Calculate rewards on a daily and weekly basis. Think of the reward as a way to pay positive attention, not as bribery. Also, don't muddy the waters by taking rewards away as punishment (unless you've been instructed in this technique by a skilled professional).

The daily totals sum up behavior over the course of the entire day, not in just one category. The weekly totals measure how well the child did during the week. If you see a pattern (such as in the Homework category in the following sample chart), then you know there's some problem-solving to do.

Does My Child Need a Behavior Chart?

Sample Chart

Desired Behavior	S	M	T	W	T	F	S
General Cooperation and Respect: Listens to and follows all house rules. Cooperates with requests. Is polite to other family members.	2	3	2				
Morning Routine: Gets up and gets dressed on time. Eats breakfast and is ready on time.	2	2	3				
Homework: Brings home all necessary materials. Completes assignments on time without delays or arguments.	1	2	1				
Daily Totals:	5	7	6				

Ratings:	Per Category:	Per Day:
Excellent	3	7-9
Good	2	4-6
Needs Improvement	1	3-5
Poor	0	0-2

Behavior in Perspective

We humans learn through trial and error. Mistakes are our greatest teachers. Yet we sometimes have the expectation that our kids should not make mistakes, or that we should shield them from the pain of natural consequences. No amount of ADHD treatment or behavior management is going to make the perfect, or close to perfect, child. Instead, we aim for more peace and quiet in our homes, closer emotional bonds that don't get stretched by daily strife, warmth, and a child who's learning to manage ADHD. How can you do this? Use the available tools. Practice forgiveness. Don't prophesize dire outcomes. Have a sense of humor.

> *No amount of ADHD treatment or behavior management is going to make the perfect child.*

Parents Press & SOS Programs have very helpful and easy to understand behavior management materials. See *www.sosprograms.com.*

Question 15

Why Does My Child Have So Many Problems in School?

No one can tell that your child has ADHD by looking at her body. Ironically, ADHD is a hidden disability with a very visible public display, especially for kids with hyperactive/impulsive (H/I) or combined type (C) disorders. In certain public settings, such as a playground, few people would think your child's behavior was especially difficult. Wow, how this story changes in school! To the *trained* teacher, your child's behavior will readily identify her as possibly having ADHD. Why is that?

Playgrounds don't require your child to display gobs of self-control or pay attention for prolonged periods of time. Sure, good sandbox skills matter, but high energy on a playground can be a valuable commodity. Scattered attention and high energy in a classroom can be a belly-up stock. Of course, the mismatch of environmental demands and your child's ADHD characteristics may lead many teachers and other school personnel to see your child as the kid who *won't* behave instead of the kid who *can* behave and perform when we make changes in the environment.

School Norms

If schools want kids who can sit at desks, face forward, speak when asked, follow written or understood rules, be obedient, and do work that often seems endless and super-boring, then kids with ADHD are in trouble. They need stimulation, lots of motivation, positive feedback, interesting work tasks, and freedom to move. While the school environment doesn't cause ADHD, it certainly asks for a lot more than most kids with this disability can give without help.

Does the Type of ADHD Make a Difference?

Each of the ADHD core symptoms brings its own set of problems. The child with predominantly inattentive ADHD may have minor problems at home and with peers. In school, where attention is a highly valued commodity, not enough attention can significantly deplete your child's learning and performance. If not understood or appropriately managed, your child may be judged rather than helped. You (and your child) may be told your child is lazy, unmotivated, or not too bright. That's name-calling in lieu of knowing how to help the child with attention problems.

> *School-based interventions are considered a vital part of ADHD management.*

The attention problems for children with the combined type often take a backseat to the very obvious impulsive and poor self-control behaviors that disrupt the class and tick off people. If your child has H/I or C type, you want to be sure that school difficulties related to inattention don't go unnoticed and unattended.

School-based interventions are considered a vital part of ADHD management. The remainder of this chapter will be about strategies for specific problems in order to help children with hyperactivity and impulsivity. The next chapter will cover inattention issues.

Hyperactive/Impulsive School Troubles

The "In High Gear" Problem

You've heard it called "motormouth" and "overdrive." The excessive motor activity of ADHD is easily seen and heard. The teacher may tell you that your child doesn't sit still, fidgets, taps anything and everything, or needs to be glued to their seat. Loud and frequent talking or other forms of verbal noise-making may be a constant disruption. The teacher may not know that the movement of ADHD, once thought to be excessive and purposeless, may actually be self-stimulation to help arouse an underaroused brain.

Moving Problems

Too much "mojo" causes the obvious problems: out of her seat more often than others; frequent or desired trips to the bathroom, water fountain, the hall, the locker, "anywhere but here in this desk and chair;" and wiggling and making noises. Also expect frequent fooling with objects, touching other students, and playing with work tools. You could see torn pages, broken pencils, exploding pens, and notebooks or worksheets that have seen better days. You could also hear the verbal motor that sounds similar to a motorcycle shifting gears, or giggling that turns into loud guffaws.

The "Hate to Wait" Problem

Part of underarousal is "untimeliness" and too much response. Kids with ADHD hate to wait! That's not a judgment call on their parts. It's the call of their nature! They don't get "later!" "Later" means we can control impulse and the need for immediate gratification in service of a higher purpose or to reap a greater and not-too-visible reward, perhaps something such as self-satisfaction. Let's be honest. Most of us without ADHD don't like to wait, either. We're just better able to say "not now."

Waiting Problems

Poor self-control shows up in so many ways, especially as difficulty using the rules to guide behavior without external support. Also expect inconsistent performance, disorganization, off-task behavior, problems completing lengthy or multistep tasks, time management issues, and poor use of study skills. You will notice the child blurting out questions or answers (often irrelevant or incorrect), hand-raising, frequent interruptions, and inappropriate comments.

You may also notice your child rushing through work (to get it done faster); missing essential information such as parts of directions, or making careless errors, especially more errors at the end of tasks, and later in the day.

Messy handwriting, math problems not correctly lined up, "hating" to read because it's boring, and reading to get it done instead of reading to understand are all seen in these types of children.

The Law of Diminishing Returns

Behavior of children with ADHD often worsens throughout the day. Think of what happens to your child. He has only so much energetic resource for self-control. Kids with ADHD get used up! Their cognitive energy depletes and needs constant replenishment.

11 Ways to Help With Self-Control

In my workshops, we trained many teachers about how to deal with students who have ADHD. Following are the general principles I train teachers to understand and apply. I've provided some examples of how to use the principles, but to be thorough, this topic requires its own book. It is important for you to have a sense of what should be happening, which is why I've included these highlights.

1. Develop a disability perspective. When teachers see your child's behavioral issues as stemming from ADHD, they are less rejecting and less likely to use angry or hostile responses. They show more empathy and willingness to help. They cultivate an accepting atmosphere that discourages the other students from being mean and rejecting. Use a problem-solving approach such as the one described in Question 10 to address social/emotional, academic, and behavioral problems.

2. Change expectations. Understand that the child with ADHD will need a lot more direct supervision than other classmates. Give the supervision with patience and cheer. Don't take behavior personally. Be forgiving. Sounds easy; does hard! But it can be done. Yes, even in a class of 25 students. Use more direct, guided instruction, and team the child with an academically competent partner whose temperament is easy and quieting. Have class rules that cover typical ADHD problem behaviors, and enforce them for all students. Expect misbehavior and don't buy into the myth that the kid is out to get you! Show forgiveness and build rapport with this child, and he will try harder in your class. Monitor ongoing problems and engage in problem-solving to address the issue.

3. Expect behavioral difficulties. Especially when work tasks are too long, too hard, or too boring. Design lessons that are shorter and interesting. Give difficult parts of tasks earlier, while the energy is still there to meet the challenges. Build confidence by giving the child tasks she can do easily and then gradually add levels of difficulty. Allow choices of tasks whenever possible, and do this with all the students. Then it won't feel like preferential treatment or "too much to do" for one child. Reuse task structures that have worked well. Build movement into lessons, especially later in the period and the day. Use stress release techniques such as breathing or gentle stretching to ease fear and frustration in more difficult tasks.

4. Think "Tom Sawyer." Work drains; play energizes. White-washing a fence can be a real bore, so make work into play! Add movement, connection, personal meaning, games, and so on. For example, each lesson can be divided into three parts: personal relevance, content mastery, and beyond-the-classroom application. Begin by determining how the content has personal relevance. For instance, volcanoes and explosive behavior have a lot in common. Personal relevance is more than a gimmick. It actually helps the brain embed new content by relating the new to the known. Next, use authentic tasks to learn new content. If studying volcanoes, have the students build models or make plans to build a model. Tie the model-building into decision-making. For instance, if you were the mayor of a town located by a volcano how would you create an evacuation plan? Finally, extend to the real world. Here the students could research evacuation plans for the town they live in.

5. Use a firewall. Wildfires can be managed with a controlled burn. Firefighters don't try to stop the fire. Instead, they clear cut boundaries so the fire becomes self-contained. If the kid with ADHD has to move, add movement to lessons and find other ways to allow movement in nondisruptive ways. For instance, some teachers give students two desks so they can switch from one to another. Some put masking tape on the floor in the back of the room so the child can pace in a confined space. Some harness the energy of this child into classroom helper and gopher.

6. Refuel. We all use cognitive energy to learn. When we need to wrestle with self-control, too, the energy depletes faster.

Think of kids with ADHD like the canaries in the mine. When they start to lose it, chances are other students are depleting, too. Their learning will also be less efficient.

Allow frequent breaks. Break tasks down into easily manageable parts. Alternate high interest/low interest tasks. Give "down time." Ease stress. Deep breathe and stretch to add oxygen and increase energy.

7. Hands on. Remember that kids with ADHD have trouble waiting and, instead, self-stimulate. Better to have stimulation on your terms. Give the child something active to do while waiting. That is, play with a rubber coated paper clip, stress ball, or sponge; use doodle paper and crayons or markers to doodle with; and build more hands-on activity into tasks.

8. Call a substitute. Children with ADHD may not understand the directions or know where to begin. Often, the teacher cannot get to the student right away. Idle times lead to disruptive behavior. So take precaution. For difficulty waiting, substitute verbal or motor responses help a lot. Teach the child to continue with easier parts, underline or rewrite directions, highlight with colored markers, or take notes.

9. Use a cue ball. Remember that kids with ADHD are managed by the moment. Similar to parents, teachers need to use visible and audible cues to help the child guide behavior, especially ones that let the child know that she needs to adjust the motor and wait.

Remind the child to use the strategies for difficulty waiting. Use silent signals and coach STAR and Stop and Think strategies described in previous chapters. Seat the child closer for more direct supervision. Cue changes in routines and transitions.

10. Make rules very clear. Posted rules help the child guide behavior, especially when they are reinforced frequently and when good behavior is acknowledged, affirmed, and appreciated rather than expected.

Refer to the rules when the child begins to lose control. Use praise and show appreciation when the child retursn to appropriate behavior or catches herself self in the act. Because the rules will lose their potency over time, take them off the wall (hopefully they've been put in a visible place), and involve the students in making a new chart and deciding where to place it. Do this every interim warning period and at the end of every marking period.

11. Feedback. The three-step method to improve performance explained in Question 11 applies to all settings and is a good template for school settings: create a structure, provide frequent feedback, and give consequences. Use lots of positive feedback. Limit negatives. Redirect or channel impulsivity and hyperactivity. Deliver behavioral correction in a respectful manner. Coach the student and cheer this student on.

These 11 guides for teachers will help. But you do need to be careful of how you approach your child's teachers with this information. Understand that your child's teachers, similar to you, are probably doing the best they can with the information, training, and belief systems they have. Share the information, but not in a demanding way that might feel bullying and controlling.

Question 16

Why Can't My Child Pay Attention All the Time?

When your child's teacher checks off the "doesn't pay attention" box on the report card, if you are like most parents, you probably have some version of this conversation with your kid.

"You need to pay attention."

"I do pay attention."

"If you paid attention, the teacher wouldn't be checking off the box."

"But I am paying attention. What's that teacher talking about?!"

Pay Attention!

Your child isn't trying to cop a plea here. If you understand that attention is a complex brain process, you'll realize that your child's lack of attention is not a conscious choice. Your child probably intends to "pay attention" but gets distracted by something else that captures his attention. He probably does not even know his mind has wandered until someone or something brings that information to his attention.

129

Unfortunately, instead of hearing "Please redirect your attention to..." your child probably hears, "You're supposed to be paying attention to...!" The first type of feedback is an observation of behavior. The "you're supposed to" feedback is a judgement and criticism often delivered with a harsh or exasperated tone. Generally, kids with ADHD get way too much of this type of condeming feedback. You can understand why they feel "picked on" or unjustly accused, especially when you understand that their attention issues are brain-based and not deliberate choices.

> *"Being inattentive means being otherwise attracted."*
> *—Ellen Langer*

How the Brain Pays Attention

When we pay attention, the brain focuses on a particular target. For instance, you are reading this book. Right now, it has your attention. But let's say you are reading at the coffee shop in your favorite bookstore. You're focused and following every word—until someone walks by with a "Double Mocha with a Hint of Hazelnut." The smell captures your attention. Your mind drifts to a pleasant afternoon you had with a friend not too long ago when you both had hazelnut coffee. You're just about to take out your cell phone and call your friend. But you are on a mission. You want to finish reading this book. You redirect your attention back to the printed page.

Within a split second, your attention went from a sustained state to alerted, oriented, and focused on something else. Then it reoriented to what you were doing and refocused on the reading. Having your mind drift is natural—in fact, it can save your life, especially if instead of a coffee aroma, you smelled something burning. The attention challenge is redirecting and sustaining it to the task at hand—particularly in the presence of appealing distractions.

ADHD Attention Issues

ADHD isn't a problem of no attention. It's a problem in one or all of the following areas:

Orienting: Is what needs attention, getting the attention? Many kids with ADHD may have trouble orienting their attention, meaning their minds are all over the place. Similar to a bee in the yard who can't quite find the flower garden amidst the bushes and trees, problems orienting attention lead to problems getting started on tasks or getting back on track when distracted.

Sustaining: Is what needs attention getting it long enough? Lack of sustained attention is also described as poor concentration, short attention span, distractibility, or a wandering mind. The executive attention network is responsible for sustained attention. It helps us say "not now" to appealing distractions. It helps us decide what the attention priority is. It's the stick-to-it network where the bee finds the flower, sucks the nectar, makes the honey, and fills the honey comb. Unlike the bee, the child with ADHD has difficulty staying focused or redirecting distracted attention to the target until no longer required.

Seekers of Stimulation

The attention issue for most kids with ADHD is that something may attract them, but the attraction doesn't last. Before too long, their minds are off to the next attraction. Why?

As researcher Ellen Langer explains, "Being inattentive means being otherwise attracted." Brains seek novelty naturally. They are always looking for what's new, interesting, or important to our survival. Though few of us get excited by dull, boring tasks, we may be able to stick with them because of some future payoff or personal satisfaction. Because kids with

ADHD don't deal with the future, they readily trade the dull and boring for the new and novel.

Remember, the underaroused brain seeks arousal. ADHD appears to be an arousal problem. Thus, these children require more stimulation. To help kids with ADHD get and stay on task, teachers (parents, too) will want to know and use the following information.

1. What's attracting the child's attention and how can we put the attraction into work tasks?

2. How can I add interest and novelty to all tasks?

Understand that novel means new, not eternally interested. Once you find something that works, know that it won't last forever! Be ready to make changes.

Adding Interest and Using Attraction

To behave better, your child needs external supports such as those mentioned in Question 15. The same holds true for paying attention. We know that novelty and interest are two critical elements that teachers need to build into the tasks of students with ADHD. Task novelty and interest don't require your child's teachers to come to class with bells, whistles, and a three-ring circus. There are simpler ways.

Connect material to the student's personal areas of interest. Kids with ADHD tend to be interested in dramatic things such as volcanic eruptions, tidal waves, and so on. Ask the child what's interesting. You will read a detailed example of how to do this in Question 15. Other ways to combat sustained attention issues are:

➲ Allow choice of tasks.

➲ Alternate high- and low-interest tasks.

➲ Break low-interest tasks into manageable chunks of time.

132

- ⊃ Use computerized games.
- ⊃ Make games out of drill- and skill-learning.
- ⊃ Eliminate as much repetition as possible.
- ⊃ Add movement.

Other Attention-Getting Techniques

Beginning tasks: The teacher wants to help the child orient and focus so the child knows what the task requires. Increase structure, prompt all directions, point out overall structure, break tasks down to single steps, color code key directions, use an attention getter, and train a routine.

Staying "on task": Kids with ADHD will not stay with things that go on for too long, are too boring, or are too routine. The teacher wants to make the task be or appear to be shorter than it is. Break tasks into smaller bites. Allow frequent breaks. Use desk exercise (such as stretching or yawning) as a way to increase energy flow. Add jokes and little rewards as tasks progress. Use homing pigeons (timers, cue cards, voice over, finger snaps, and so on). to call the attention back should it wander. Frequent feedback along the way helps a lot, especially positive feedback. Limit lecture time.

Completing tasks: These kids will stay on task as long as they can, but sometimes they need an extra boost to finish—such as a reward. Sometimes it appears that they haven't finished because they've misplaced the work, thrown it out by mistake, or forgot to hand it in. Teachers want to make sure the problem is not disorganization. Teachers may also want to allow students to use different types of final products for task completion, such as PowerPoint, drawings, collages, and so on.

ADHD and Executive Functions

In addition to attention difficulties, researchers find that approximately 1/3 of children with ADHD also have executive function difficulties. Executive functions are complex mental processes that help us think, plan, problem-solve, organize, make decisions, manage time, and say "Not now" so that we stick to the goal in mind and get the job done. Though more obvious during adolescence, these problem-solving and decision-making skills are evident even in preschoolers.

EFs are similar to brain bosses that supervise the workers who handle the piles of "work" we have to do as life and tasks become increasingly complex. The bosses create structured work environments where all the workers know what they have to do to reach their goals and objectives efficiently.

The brain area most involved with executive functions is the prefrontal cortex (PFC). The PFC is also one of the key brain areas affected by ADHD. Children with ADHD will need help from outside executives to supervise the many brain activities regulated by the executive functions. Many of the management techniques already mentioned in this book help with executive functioning.

These techniques fall into four categories:

- **Structure**: Needs to be consistent, predictable, individualized, caring, and intentionally flexible. Consists of anything done externally, such as rules, feedback, schedules, task-design, and so on.

- **Skills**: May not be learned or their use may need to be prompted. To teach skills, follow these steps— model, practice, evaluate, give feedback, correct, and reward.

- **Strategies**: We change what we do to meet the child's needs: microsize, "act—don't react," do the step by step, use direct guided instruction, use behavior management, medication, timers, daily planners, homework notebooks, and so on.

- **Supports:** That extra pair of hands that guides and encourages. Supports add motivation, recognize success, provide signposts, do on-site problem-solving, and provide frequent feedback. Tutors can be very helpful in showing your child how to manage tasks. They have the added value of instructing your child in skill gaps caused by inattention.

Using This Information

As a parent, you walk a slippery slope when it comes to working with your child's teacher(s). Many take offense if they think you are teaching them how to teach. They usually want your support, but often don't know exactly what that means.

Give them this book. It will help them better understand ADHD and know what to do about ADHD school-related problems.

When a teacher calls you about a problem, don't let the call be a vent-off! Brainstorm and look for solutions. Don't get snarled in jams about your child's "disruptive" behavior. Identify learning and performance problems. Focus on the ways you and the teacher can help your child in these areas. Remember: If your child is actively engaged in an interesting task, he won't need to be disruptive.

Question 17

How Do I Work with My Child's Teachers?

In the teacher training workshops I do on ADHD, I always begin with this fill-in-the-blank exercise: ADHD is like____. When I designed this exercise, I knew it would be a springboard to all the negative beliefs teachers had about ADHD. Though those negative beliefs do pop out, interestingly, many teachers have filled in the blank with ADHD's positive aspects: high energy, creativity, interesting perspectives, spontaneity, and eager to help.

Our attitudes reflect our beliefs. These drive our actions. Clearly, your child will do better with teachers who understand and appreciate your child's attributes and ADHD challenges and who have received training in teaching students with ADHD.

A Disability Perspective

Teachers with disability perspective see the problems caused by ADHD with nonjudgmental eyes. They seeks to solve problems, not to place blame or to punish the child. They understand that in order for a child to be responsible, the adults must

136

help the child develop response-ability. They know that these children can do, but not without recognition, understanding, guidance, and skill. They build on strengths and possibilities.

Some teachers confuse a disability perspective with lowering standards. For instance, while doing a teacher training, I met a teacher who refused to make accommodations for any student. He prided himself on his standards. He didn't mean to be callous or insensitive. His beliefs, however, got in the way of his good intention, which was to have his students feel a genuine sense of accomplishment when they completed his class. From his point of view, the only way students could truly appreciate an accomplishment was to walk the high wire of his standards without a net and to suffer the consequences of any fall.

During the workshop, a miracle happened. His eyes opened to a disability perspective. He saw, perhaps for the first time, that making task accommodations for kids with ADHD is no different than providing wheelchair ramps for kids who can't walk. How do I know? He had to leave the workshop to attend a parent/teacher conference. Much to his supervisor's surprise, he actually came up with things he could do to help the student, including extra time on tests—something he had never allowed for anybody.

> *For a child to be responsible, the adults must help the child develop response-ability.*

Teachers Who Don't Understand

Imagine if I had hammered this teacher about his insensitivity and lack of awareness. What if I blamed or called him to task in front of his peers? That type of response may have set this teacher to dig his heels in farther.

Teachers are no different than the rest of the population. They come in all sizes, shapes, and temperaments. Some truly believe that making accommodations is a disservice or is unfair to other students. Others buy into the many myths of ADHD. Some don't connect the dots. Some simply lack training.

Isn't It Ironic?

You expect the teacher to be the expert and to know how to manage ADHD in the classroom. Often, they turn to you for ideas and suggestions. The teacher may also expect you to send your child to school ready, willing, and able to learn as well as to handle the school problems at home. Unrealistic expectations can send us into a playing field where no one wins.

You May Get Ticked Off!

If you feel your child is being mishandled, naturally you're going to get upset and possibly reactive. That's a parental instinct. Honor your instinct, but whatever you do, don't take "attitude" to school. It won't serve your child. In fact, teachers may use your "attitude" as proof that you aren't a supportive or able parent. What can you do? Count to 10, hit golf balls, or go for a brisk walk. But be in control when you talk to school personnel.

The Blame Game

In my travels, I see far too many instances where teachers blame parents and vice versa. Meanwhile, there's a child in need, falling between the pointing fingers. Blame lures us into thinking we're taking action. We're not. We're reacting. Whether you are the parent or the teacher, when you blame, you're basically saying, "It's in your hands because I don't know what to do and shouldn't be expected to find out."

If you find that you've fallen into this type of interaction, there's something you can do. It takes two to keep a blame game going. If you want to change the game, drop out. Move into problem-solving mode. You'll feel much more productive.

How to Be Your Child's Advocate

➲ **Be knowledgeable and stay informed.** Most teachers appreciate your clearheaded understanding of your child's problems and any possible interventions you can suggest. Read and keep up to date on new research.

➲ **Use knowledge to help, not to hammer.** Knowledge helps create solutions for problems. But sometimes knowledge can be used to beat up on people who "should know better." That's like calling someone a "stupid idiot." You want to help by sharing your knowledge.

➲ **Speak up, not out.** Good communication skills are crucial for effective advocacy. Always be polite and respectful, even of people who don't seem to warrant your respect. Act as if they might rise to the occasion one day. Be aware of your tone, volume, and body language. Don't make accusations. If you feel you're going to lose it, excuse yourself. Nothing gets solved during a shouting match.

➲ **Know your intention.** Before meetings, have an agenda. What are your child's needs? What do you hope to accomplish? Is there a specific problem that needs attention? Put your energy there.

➲ **Stay focused on your intention.** Don't get sidetracked by emotional issues that may come up in conferences or phone calls. Either you or the school personnel have an agenda. Stick to the agenda, solving problems, and meeting needs. The meeting will move more smoothly.

➲ **Use conflict resolution skills.** Don't get too invested in the belief that your way is the only way. Conflict resolution is a negotiation. Both parties have perspectives and issues that belong on the table. Look for ways to solve the table topics that create wins for all. Avoid the "I win/you lose" agenda.

➲ **Bring a skilled advocate to meetings.** It can be intimidating to deal with school staff on your own, especially when you're first learning about ADHD and feel as though you are in over your head. Parent/child advocates can help you. Look to your local disability support groups to find these names. Find your local disability support groups by reading newspaper calendars, asking school personnel or your child's treatment professionals, or by searching the Web.

➲ **Keep good records.** Get a large three-ring binder. Fill it with records of anything pertaining to school: report cards, meetings, phone contacts, evaluations, intervention plans, and so on.

Listen to Your Child—But Not 100%

Sally slammed the front door. "MOM, you won't believe what Mrs. So and So did today. I'm telling you, she's out to get me. She is always yelling at me for stupid things I didn't do. She calls on me when she knows I don't know the answer just to embarrass me in front of the class. I'm never going back there. MOM! You've got to do something," she said.

Sound vaguely familiar? We know there are teachers who are control freaks. We know some teachers can be emotionally abusive, whether or not they intend to be. We also know that kids with ADHD view the world from their unique and often reactive perspective. They tend to blow off steam in a very dramatic and alarming way. Then they go out to shoot hoops and leave you stirred up and looking to shoot!

140

Clearly, if your child has major and ongoing complaints about a particular teacher or teachers, don't assume anything. Investigate. Claims are warning signals. It may be the teacher. It may be that your child's feeling incapable of doing the work. It may be a misunderstanding. Regardless, a peaceful rapport needs to be established; otherwise, the year can be pretty awful.

Teacher Traits That Help ADHD

In ADHD circles, we hear this lament over and over: "Last year my child had a teacher who knew what to do, and my child did really well. This year the teacher doesn't want to know about his ADHD and he's having a terrible year." We know kids with ADHD tend to do better with certain types of teachers. If at all possible, you will want to work with guidance counselors and the principal to have your child placed with teachers who have the following traits:

⊃ **Use a lot of encouragement and praise.** This trait is actually a habit that reflects an inner positive attitude. Teachers with this habit make a lot of affirming statements: "Great job," "Good try," and "Mistakes are okay here." One way a teacher can gauge how much positive feedback she gives is to keep a jar of pennies on the desk. The teacher can then give a penny to the student along with a positive comment. At the end of the day, if the jar is too full, that means it's time to work on this positive habit. These teachers also know the student's strengths and work on creating opportunities for the student to shine.

⊃ **Appreciate and recognize student effort.** These teachers don't wait for final products, but comment on progress and steps mastered along the way. Grading systems include marks for handing in work and for the effort put into it in addition to getting the answers right. They decorate papers with stickers,

141

and have special incentive programs. For example, four days of homework in on time and the student gets the fifth day off.

➲ **Highly structured and organized, but not rigid.** These teachers post rules, schedules, and homework assignments in the same place. They set aside specific periods for specific tasks and provide regularly scheduled and frequent breaks. These teachers use cues and other attention-getting devices and ease transitions between activities. They establish routine systems for handing out and collecting work. They make classroom behavior and work expectations clear, and they reinforce them with positive feed-back. These teachers are also intentionally flexible when the system needs to give a little. They create comprehensive lesson plans that actively engage the student.

➲ **Patient, and willing to take extra time.** These teachers help the student with organization. They repeat directions as necessary. Directions are also given one at a time. They check to make sure the student is paying attention and understands the material. They also help the student organize and and stay organized on a daily basis.

➲ **High stress tolerance/low reactivity.** These teachers respond calmly to inappropriate behavior. They create a safe classroom atmosphere absent of ridicule, yelling, and other reactive behaviors. They deliver consequences in a calm, matter-of-fact way. They practice stress management techniques in the classroom.

➲ **Make accommodations.** These teachers make accommodations specific to the student's individual needs. Common ADHD accomodations are prefer-ential seating (close to the teacher and away from distractions), allowing extra time when needed, using computerized instruction, and reducing the amount of homework, breaking down large tasks into smaller ones and providing an extra set of notes or note-taking buddy. These teachers use different types of assessments to measure mastery of content and also use word banks and other devices to help students with working memory problems retrieve information for tests.

➲ Modifies curriculum. These teachers provide tasks of high interest and motivation and limit the amount of lecture time to curb boredom. They use a lot of hands-on, authentic, and meaningful tasks. They plan academic subjects in the morning hours (elementary school) and alternate activities to eliminate desk fatigue.

➲ See challenges as opportunities. Similar to using frequent praise, viewing challenges with an optimistic attitude is a habit. Teachers with this habit feel competent about their teaching abilities, use problem-solving responses rather than knee-jerk reactions, and are not afraid to risk a new approach.

➲ Problem-solves. Whether it's a "behavior" problem or an academic difficulty, a responsive teacher uses a basic problem-solving model: analyze and identify the problem, brainstorm, try the best shot, evaluate its effectiveness, and go back to the drawing board if need be. These teachers do not give up!

➲ Work with parents and other support staff. These teachers encourage parent involvement, are skilled in conflict resolution methods, understand the parental pressures and limitations, and work with special educators or other support staff for a comprehensive approach.

143

By the way, all students benefit from teachers with these traits. Just as with parent who lack skills, students without special needs will generally do okay with a teacher lacking some or many of these traits. But kids with ADHD will have a harder time. Teachers without these skills may be more reactive and their actions more misguided. Don't mistake a lack of skill as a lack of caring and empathy. My experience as a former teacher shows me that a noncaring teacher is rare to the breed. Most teachers care a lot!

Guidelines for Parent/Teacher Contacts

You will want to develop a working relationship with your child's teachers early in the school year. Unless there's something that needs to happen right away, give teachers a few weeks to get to know your child.

When you do meet:

- ⊃ Be courteous and respectful—not demanding.
- ⊃ Appreciate the teacher's extra efforts. (Don't have an "entitled" attitude.)
- ⊃ Give the teacher time to share his/her concerns and attempts to solve the problem.
- ⊃ Offer information. Don't preach!

Question 18 ?

Does My Child Need Special Education?

Your child *may* need special education. It depends on how severely ADHD impacts her educational performance, which includes social, emotional, behavioral, and academic functioning.

Children with disabilities have rights to special education services under two federal laws that states must follow: the Individuals with Disabilities Education Act (IDEA) and Section 504 of the Rehabilitation Act. You will want to learn more about these laws than space in this book allows. See the appendix for a list of advocacy Websites.

Following is very basic information. It comes from the ADHD Briefing Paper that I wrote for the National Information Center for Children and Youth with Disabilities (NICHCY). The text is taken word for word except for slight changes made for clarification and formatting purposes.

Will Special Education Help My Child?

Under the IDEA, *special education* is instruction that is specially designed (at no cost to parents) to meet the unique

145

needs of a child with a disability. "Specially designed" means adapting the content, methodology, or delivery of instruction (as appropriate) to the needs of the child, in order to:

➲ Address the unique needs of the child that result from his or her disability.

➲ Ensure the child's access to the general curriculum (the same curriculum as for students without disabilities) so that she can meet the educational standards that apply to all children within the school district or jurisdiction.

Because special education is specially designed instruction, it may be very helpful to your child. However, not all children with ADHD need, or are eligible for, special education services. Conversely, many would not be able to receive an appropriate education *without* special education services.

Some school districts take the position that ADHD *is not a qualifying* condition under the law. They couldn't be more wrong.

How Is My Child Eligible for IDEA?

The process by which a child is found eligible for special education services is described within the federal law known as the Individuals with Disabilities Education Act, or IDEA. IDEA is the federal law under schools that:

➲ Evaluate children for the presence of a disability and their need for special services.

➲ Provide special education and related services to students who meet eligibility requirements.

Eligibility decisions about a child's need for special education and related services are made on a case-by-case basis. School districts may not arbitrarily refuse to either evaluate or offer services to students with ADHD.

If your child has ADHD and it is adversely affecting his educational performance, the law requires the school to evaluate your child and provide necessary services if your child is found eligible. They cannot take a "wait and see how bad it gets" approach either. Children with disabilities must not "fail first" in order to be evaluated.

Does an ADHD Diagnosis Automatically Make My Child Eligible?

In order for your child to be eligible, he must have a disability according to the criteria set forth in IDEA or under state law (state law is based on IDEA). The disability must adversely affect his educational performance. Thus, a medical diagnosis of ADHD alone is not enough to make your child eligible for services. Educational performance, which consists of social, emotional, behavioral, or academic performance, must be adversely affected.

Presently, IDEA lists 13 categories of disability under which a child may be found eligible for special education. ADHD is specifically mentioned in the IDEA as part of its definition of "Other Health Impairment."

IDEA defines "other health impairment" as having limited strength, vitality, or alertness—including a heightened alertness to environmental stimuli—that results in limited alertness with respect to the educational environment, due to chronic or acute health problems, such as asthma, attention deficit disorder, or attention deficit hyperactivity disorder.

Children with ADHD may also be eligible under any other category for which they meet the definition.

Steps to Determine IDEA Eligibility

1. The child must be experiencing educational performance problems.

2. When such problems become evident, the parent, teacher, or another school staff person must request that the child be evaluated for the presence of a disability.

3. The child is evaluated to determine if she does indeed have a disability and to determine the nature and extent of the child's need for special education and related services.

4. A group of individuals, including the parents, meets to review the evaluation results and determine if the child meets eligibility criteria set forth in state and federal law. If so, the child is found eligible for special education and related services.

The Individualized Education Plan

If your child is found eligible for special education, you will then collaborate with school personnel to develop what is known as an Individualized Education Program (IEP). Your child's IEP is a written document that spells out, among other things, how your child's specific problems and unique learning needs will be addressed. The IEP considers strengths as well.

Positive Behavior Interventions

If a child's behavior impedes learning (including the learning of others), the parents and school must consider, if appropriate, strategies to address that behavior. This includes positive behavioral interventions, strategies, and supports. This proactive approach to addressing behavior problems is intended to help individual students minimize discipline problems that may arise as a result of the disability. If your child has behavior problems, you will want to make sure that these are addressed in his or her IEP.

Be sure your child's IEP also addresses any academic performance and learning problems. It's too easy to see the behavior problems of ADHD and not focus on these other critical issues.

IEP Services

After specifying the nature of your child's special needs, the IEP team (which includes you) determines what types of services are appropriate for addressing those needs. The IEP team also decides where your child will receive these services—for example, the regular education classroom, a resource room, or a separate classroom.

For Further Information

The IEP is a very important document in the lives of students with disabilities. There is a lot to know about how it is developed, what type of information it contains, and what part you, as a parent, play in writing it. More detailed information about the IEP process is available from NICHCY at (800) 695-0285 or *www.nichcy.org*.

What If My Child Is Not Eligible for IDEA Services?

Under IDEA, the school system must tell you in writing why your child was found "not eligible." It must also give you information about what you can do if you disagree with this decision. There are legal actions and remedies available. Each state has specific procedures required by IDEA that must be followed.

Read the information the school system gives you. Make sure it includes information about how to challenge the eligibility decision. If that information is not in the materials the school gives you, ask the school for it.

Also, get in touch with your state's Parent Training and Information (PTI) center. PTI can tell you what steps to take next. Your PTI is listed on NICHCY's *State Resource Sheet* for your state. (See Website.)

149

Section 504

It is also helpful to know that students with ADHD may be eligible for services under a different law—Section 504 of the Rehabilitation Act of 1973. Section 504 is a civil rights law prohibiting discrimination on the basis of a disability. Any school district that receives federal funds must follow this law.

> *Students with ADHD may be eligible for services under Section 504.*

Under Section 504, a person with a disability means any person with an impairment that "substantially limits one or more major life activities." Since learning is considered a major life activity, many students with ADHD qualify as a "person with a disability" under Section 504. Schools are then required to provide them with a "free appropriate public education," which can include regular or special education services, depending upon each student's specific needs.

Therefore, if your child is found ineligible for services under IDEA, ask to have your child evaluated under the criteria of Section 504. Many children are not eligible for services under IDEA but *are* eligible under Section 504.

Also know that many schools will try to provide a 504 plan in lieu of doing an IDEA evaluation. Legally, if they suspect that your child has a disability that adversely affects educational performance, they are required under IDEA'S Child Find and under Section 504 to do an evaluation.

Question 19

?

What Can Be Done About Homework Horrors?

If you want to explain to others what homework is like when your child has ADHD tell them to read a Stephen King novel—*Misery* would do just fine. As parents, we get a double whammy—watching our kids feel miserable and having their misery become ours. Talk about a source of parent/child conflict!

Homework—What's the Real Problem?

Homework requires your child to be organized, and to have all the necessary materials, plus know what to do and how to do it. It means that your child must call forth cognitive energy, which is no doubt depleted from the day he had at school. This energy needs to be used in the service of an often unpleasant, unrewarding, dull, or boring task. And there are so many appealing distractions that get in the way. No wonder many kids with ADHD consider homework a form of legalized torture!

You may find homework also creates stress for you. Maybe you feel pressure because it takes a lot from you to see that your child gets the homework done. You may worry about how homework will affect your child's school success, and perhaps even college possibilities.

Take heart. There are many ways to stop the madness. Some are child-centered. Others have to do with the actual homework. Let's begin there. Find out:

1. Is it really homework? The teacher may occasionally send home uncompleted classwork for your child to finish if there's a good reason. If the teacher has made a regular practice of expecting your child to finish school work at home, then that situation needs attention. Make sure homework is truly homework—something given outside of class that supports the learning going on in class.

2. Is it too much, too boring, or taking too long? If the homework is skill-and-drill stuff, your child will probably get bored very easily. The in-school rules about tedious tasks apply to homework, too. Cut the work down (for example, do even-numbered problems only). If your child knows and successfully uses the skill, the teacher can be encouraged not to make your child "prove" it over and over. If the tasks are too long, break them into manageable bites. Always contact the teacher if there is a problem.

3. Is it counterproductive? Why is homework given? Is it an old habit pattern or belief system? Teachers have been known to assign homework because they think it instills discipline, or because their school administrator believes kids should spend X-amount of time doing homework.

Be aware that homework can cause problems, especially if your child's learning a skill and making mistakes during the practice part. It's much harder to unlearn than it is to learn.

Perhaps you can work with your school's parent/teacher organization to be sure that homework is meaningful, necessary, academically sound, and enhancing.

Dealing With Homework Problems

The following interventions are child-centered. They examine typical problems children with ADHD experience with legitimate homework and offer suggestions for solving those problems.

➲ **I don't have any homework!** Your child may not have gotten the assignment, may not have written it down, or simply forgotten it under the "out of sight, out of mind" scenario typical of ADHD.

What to do: Use a homework planner. Ask the teacher to check that homework is written down (along with due dates for upcoming projects and tests.)Be sure the homework planner gets into your child's backpack and home.

➲ **I'm sure I put what I needed in here!** Missing materials necessary to do the homework is almost a given.

What to do: Use a "bring home" folder. Send necessary papers by e-mail attachment. Have a back-up buddy. Keep an extra set of books and all other school supplies at home. Have someone supervise the loading of the backpack at day's end.

➲ **I'll be there in a minute!** Expect procrastination and resistance, unless it's something really cool that the child can easily do. Often, it takes our children longer to do their assignments than other kids. Reading can be especially painful because they are not doing something active.

What to do: Have a regularly scheduled time to be at a specific place. Provide incentives for getting there on time and rewards for staying there. Avoid money rewards. Use privileges or material objects. Think encouragement and enrollment, not bribery!

➲ **What am I supposed to do?** Your child may not understand the requirements, the directions, or have the necessary skills to do the task.

What to do: Find out the basis for the problem. For requirements and directions, call a buddy. For necessary skills, try until frustration begins, then ask the teacher to give your child extra help.

➲ **Oh my god! I have a book report due tomorrow.** It's a little late for even foxhole prayers at this point. How many of us have stayed up all night, typed the "due in the morning" term paper, and so on. Parents, this is crazy! And totally unnecessary.

What to do: Long-term projects should be written down and broken down into smaller tasks that can be easily completed step-by-step at a reasonable pace. I trained my students to write long-term assignments in each day of their daily homework planners until the due date. They also made notes about when they handed in sections. Teachers are the checkpoint to be sure that assignments get in the planner and progress is made on schedule. Parents are the home backup to monitor and supervise their completion. Teachers can also use e-mail to directly notify parents about long-term assignments.

➲ **I left it at home!** What a pity to have done the work and gotten no credit. Usually this happens because there's no routine for getting the work back to school.

What to do: Have an object-placement routine—perhaps a special completed homework folder that is used for all subjects. Load your child's backpack the night before. Leave it in the same place. Check to see that leaves the house with your child.

154

Guidelines to Develop Homework Responsibility

Eventually, your child needs to develop responsibility for homework. There are some techniques that will train your child, and some things that will make this misery more manageable.

➲ Have structure and routine—same time, same place, stocked supplies.

➲ Schedule oxygen breaks. Timed and frequent breaks remove tension and recharge the brain. Use timers so your child isn't negotiating with you.

➲ Allow stimulation. Many children with ADHD work better with background music to filter distractions. Some need to do something with their hands, too.

➲ Make a checklist for following directions and completing and putting work back into the school folder.

➲ Give immediate rewards.

➲ Monitor completion. Especially with older children, you don't want to correct homework or teach—unless you are absolutely invited. The teacher needs to know what your child understood. In most situations, homework should be practice and not a quiz grade.

➲ Use a weekly homework chart with daily accounting. (These are similar to behavior charts: Has assignments written down, starts on time, follows the schedule, completes the work without too much complaint, puts completed work in proper place. Give points to earn rewards.)

➲ Get out of the line of fire. Tutors and in-school homework programs can be great ways to eliminate your exposure to conflict and stress.

Question 20

Will My Child Become a Responsible Adult?

In the previous pages, you've been exposed to lots of information and strategies to help you help your child. Still, the day will come when your child will be an adult. How can you help your child prepare for his or her future?

Train Self-Advocacy

Involve your child in all aspects of the care and tending of his life. Have your child be an important member of the team that discovers his strengths, talents, and abilities. Encourage your child to learn about ADHD and to keep the disorder in perspective.

When problems arise, have your child be an equally vested partner in search of solutions. Help him learn to recognize his needs and to find healthy, adaptive ways to fill those needs.

Teach your child to speak up, not out; to discuss problems and issues with others; to work with and not against the tide.

Effective advocacy whether you are the parent or the emerging adult with ADHD requires a cool, calm, collected approach.

Understand that no life is problem-free. Teach your child to get going when the going gets rough. To get going is not the same as running away. By taking action, by using all the treatment options available, your child will learn to run to meet situations. Part of the way a parent helps a child "run to and not away" comes from allowing some degree of struggle.

Encourage Emergence

Think of the butterfly struggling to break through the cocoon. Any of us might be tempted to ease the butterfly's struggle by helping it to break out. We might believe that to do so would be an act of kindness. But butterflies need to go through that struggle to build the strength necessary to survive in adulthood. If we intervene in that process, we deprive the butterfly of a very vital stage of development.

> *Parents do what they can to prepare an ADHD-friendly cocoon for their children.*

As children move through their cocoons, our roles as parents emerge as well. In a sense, we do what we can to prepare an ADHD-friendly cocoon for them. And then we stand alongside, offering encouragement and support. As they work through their struggles, they emerge into able adults who learn how to meet their needs.

ADHD may be a tough cocoon, but many children with this problem have learned to do much more than manage their lives. They've learned to appreciate the richness of life. Will your child become a responsible adult? There's every reason to believe so.

157

Additional Information

Websites

In addition to the Websites referred to previously, these other sites may be helpful:

www.ldonline.com

www.nami.org   National Alliance for Mentally Ill

www.nmha.org   National Mental Health Association Resource Center

www.aacap.org   American Academy of Child and Adolescent Psychiatry

www.aap.org   American Academy of Pediatrics

www.ldanatl.org   Learning Disabilities Association of America

www.ffcmh.org   Federation of Families for Children's Mental Health

www.adaa.org   Anxiety Disorders Association of America

www.cabf.org   Adolescent Bipolar Foundation

Disability Rights and Special Education Information:

www.bazelon.org

www.usdoj.gov

www.ed.gov

www.wrightslaw.com

www.reedmartin.com

www.ncgiadd.org (for gender issues and ADHD)

Books

For more information about ADHD, these books will be helpful. Find them online or at your local bookstore.

For Parents

Barkley, R. *Taking Charge of ADHD, Revised Edition.* New York: Guilford Press, 2000.

Brooks, R. and S. Goldstein. *Raising Resilient Children.* New York: Contemporary Books, 2001.

Fowler, M. *Maybe You Know My Kid: A Parent's Guide for Identifying, Understanding, and Helping Your Child with ADHD, Third Edition.* New York: Kensington Press, 1999.

Fowler, M. *Maybe You Know My Teen, A Parent's Guide to Helping Your Adolescent with ADHD.* New York: Broadway Books, 2001.

Jensen, P. *Making the System Work for Your Child with ADHD.* New York: Guilford Press, 2004.

Katz, Mark. *Playing a Poor Hand Well.* New York: W.W. Norton, Inc., 1996.

Lavoie, R. *It's So Much Work to Be Your Friend.* New York: Simon and Schuster, 2005.

Nadeau, K., and E. Littman, and P. Quinn. *Understanding Girls with AD/HD*. Silver Spring, Md.: Advantage Books, 1999.

Wilens, T. *Straight Talk About Psychiatric Medications for Kids*. New York: Guilford Press, 1998.

For Adults

Hallowell, E. and J. Ratey. *Delivered from Distraction*. New York: Ballantine Books, 2005.

Hallowell, E., and J. Ratey. *Driven to Distraction*. New York: Simon and Schuster, 1995.

Kelly, K. and P. Ramundo. *You Mean I'm Not Lazy, Stupid, or Crazy!* Cincinnati, Ohio: Tyrell & Jerem Press,1993.

For children

Clark, L. *SOS: Help for Emotions*. Bowling Green, Ky: Parents Press, 1996.

Galvin, M. *Otto Learns About His Medicine*. Washington, D.C.: American Psychological Association, 1995.

Gordon, M. *I Would If I Could*. Dewitt, New York: Gordon Systems, 1992.

Moss, D. *Shelly, The Hyperactive Turtle*. Rockville, Md.: Woodbine House, 1992.

Parker, R. *Making the Grade*. Plantation, Fla: Speciality Press, 1992.

Quinn, P. and J. Stern. *Putting on the Brakes: Young People's Guide to Understanding Attention Deficit Hyperactivity Disorder*, Washington, D.C.: American Psychological Association, 1991.

Newsletters and Periodicals

ADHD Briefing Paper, *www.nichcy.org* or *maryfowler.com* (copyright free 28 page guide to ADHD).